A Billion Gods and Goddesses:
The Mythology Behind
the Pipe Woman Chronicles
Second Edition

Lynne Cantwell

hearth/myth

Table of Contents

Introduction

"Mythology" is what we call someone else's religion.

Joseph Campbell, *The Masks of God*

Nearly everybody has a hobby of some sort. One of mine is mythology – which is weirder than some, but not as weird as a lot of others.

My interest in the subject started as an adjunct to a search for my roots. A lot of Americans go through this phase, I think; almost all of us are mutts to some degree, with numerous nationalities and/or ethnicities on both sides of our family trees. Some people scratch the itch by getting into genealogy: digging ever deeper into family history, poring over census records and ship manifests. I started down that road, and then realized that much of the land had already been plowed by my relatives. A distant cousin on my father's side, Henry Vincent Cantwell, had traced the family back to the first of our line in America: Captain Edmund Cantwell, a big deal in colonial Delaware both before and after its split from Pennsylvania. Capt. Cantwell was born in Ireland, or maybe England; he helmed one of four English ships that arrived in New York when it was still a Dutch colony in 1644, took a Dutch wife, and had a passel of kids. Like all good Americans, my Cantwell forebears migrated – to Maryland, then to South Carolina, Kentucky, Indiana, Wisconsin, and Michigan, and married people of other nationalities: Irish mostly, but also English, German, and one of the Native American tribes of Michigan.

My mother's side of the family is complicated in a different way. Around the turn of the 20th century, my maternal grandparents emigrated with their families from what was then Czechoslovakia, and settled near Chicago. End of story, pretty much, unless I wanted to hire someone in the Czech Republic to search the vital records there.

Anyway, in perusing these genealogies, I discovered that names and dates are dry without any context. I'm a storyteller. I wanted to know more about these people than I could learn from land grants and baptism records. I wanted to know their customs. I wanted to know what they believed.

Around the same time, I began looking into the American Druid organization called Ár nDraíocht Féin (mercifully abbreviated, for those of us who have nae the Gaelic, as ADF). Ultimately, I decided against joining, but one of the things that intrigued me about ADF was their practice of adopting a hearth culture: devoting yourself to the gods from your ancestors' neck of the woods. ADF strongly suggests that you pick a single hearth culture rather than a smorgasbord. That was a problem for me; while I'm half Czech, I also identify strongly with the Celts (who, after all, spent some time in the Czech lands on their way across Europe – and of course my father's side is pretty heavily Irish) and the Norse (some of whom became Norman French, invaded England with William the Conqueror, and later went to Ireland with Strongbow). And then there's whichever Native American tribe my Cantwell relatives had married into.

Spiritually, it was a puzzlement. But investigating all the various pantheons brought me to the myths. Here, at last, were the stories I had been looking for, and I began to gobble them up. I started with the Celts, because they were the most accessible. Then the Slavs. Then, to a lesser degree, the Norse. And of course, the various Native American tribes.

If you've read the *Pipe Woman Chronicles*, you see where this is going.

The title of this book comes from *Seized*, the first novel in the series. Naomi Witherspoon's initial meeting with White Buffalo Calf Pipe Woman takes place on a featureless plain. The sky above them is studded with what appear to be a billion stars – but when Naomi looks closer, she realizes each star is, or represents, a god or goddess.

Over the course of the series, we get to meet a few of Them. But I couldn't pack the novels with everything about each deity that I'd gleaned from my research, and some gods got very little background information in the books at all. So when a fellow author suggested that I write a book like this, I realized it would be a great way to share some of the material I couldn't get into the series.

You say "myth" like it's a bad thing

In this book, I use the word *myth* in the anthropological sense. To most people these days, *myth* is a derogatory term that denotes a story based on a lie. But to anthropologists, a *myth* is simply a sacred narrative. The term defines everything from the Bible, to oral narratives from Micronesia, to George Washington and his cherry tree. You can extend this concept into the present day. Authors of fan fiction treat their source material – their "canon" – as a sacred narrative. People hired to write Star Wars and Star Trek novels have to stick to the myth, too.

One thing that became apparent to me, as I read my own cultural myths and then read about mythology in general, is that no matter what culture we're talking about, myths do two things: they explain the world in terms people can understand, and they pass on rules for survival within the culture. Even the funny stories – the legends about Coyote and Raven, for example – are not told just for the sake of entertainment. In an interview in *Ute Indian Arts and Culture*, Dr. James A. Goss said, "What we consider just little fairy tales or just-so stories are loaded with what we call ethical teachings. And that's the way the traditional mores or standards for behavior were passed on from generation to generation." Goss goes on to tell a story about Older Coyote and Younger Coyote getting in trouble on a hunting trip. When the boys make camp for the night, Older Coyote tells Younger Coyote to stay in camp. But even though they can hear the cannibal spirit Unupits crashing around outside their camp, Younger Coyote goes out anyway – and of course, Unupits eats him. The next morning, Older Coyote goes home to tell their father, Mountain Lion, what happened. They're both very sad, of course, but still, Mountain Lion takes his surviving son back up the mountain to where Younger Coyote disappeared. That night, Mountain Lion battles Unupits and kills him. And in the morning, the father cuts open the body of the cannibal spirit and brings Younger Coyote back to life.

So where's the lesson? Well, for one thing, Younger Coyote didn't listen to his brother and it killed him; in other words, do what your elders tell you to do. Also, don't leave camp at night in the mountains. It's too dangerous – and not just because of cannibal spirits. You could fall off a cliff in the dark.

Rules for living. Kind of like God handing Moses those stone tablets.

Some of our handy-dandy features

My intention is not to produce a scholarly work, but to provide a companion volume to the twelve books of the *Pipe Woman Chronicles* cycle, for those readers who are interested in learning more about the gods and goddesses in the books. You won't find footnotes, but I have included a bibliography in case you're interested in reading further.

In addition to the regular table of contents, I've created an alphabetized list to help you keep track of which deity is linked to which character – because I wouldn't expect anybody else to be able to keep track of the forty-odd deities/spirits/what-have-you who have found Their way into my books. The list also gives the deity's pantheon and the book in which He or She made His or Her debut. That same information has been included in every deity's section of the book.

I also hope that this slim volume might serve as a first look at mythology in general, for those who are looking for a not-too-tough introduction to the subject. And – all right, I admit it – I also nurture a tiny hope that a reader interested in mythology might pick up this book and be intrigued enough to read the novels.

I haven't included any pictures of the gods here. But I have put together several Pinterest boards devoted to the gods and goddesses who make appearances in the series, and you can find them all at http://pinterest.com/LynneCantwell.

The World Tree

Anthropologists have created several broad classifications for myths. Creation myths, as you might expect, explain how the world was formed; these fall into several sub-classifications, which I'll get into in the next section.

Mythologies are also classified by how their world is organized – and surprisingly (or at least, it surprised me), a lot of mythological systems are organized along the lines of a belief in a World Tree. Perhaps the most well-known World Tree is the one in Norse mythology, which is called Yggdrasil: the gods live at the top of the tree, the underworld is at the bottom, and our world is the part in between. Slavic mythology shares the same imagery: their gods live in Prav, at the top of the tree; Veles oversees the land of the dead in Nav, below the tree's roots; and humanity lives in the middle, in Yav.

The tripartite theme also shows up in cultures whose mythologies don't center around a World Tree. Celtic tradition, for instance, splits creation into three parts, although theirs is organized in a slightly different way; it's the gods, the Tuatha Dé Danaan, who live "under the hill," while the dead go off to the West, over the sea. Greek and Roman mythology puts the gods atop Mount Olympus, while Hades/Pluto manages the underworld. And of course, for Christians, God is in Heaven above, and the devil lives below in Hell.

You might think it odd that so many of these disparate mythologies share a similar organizational model. But all of them are considered to be Indo-European, with a common root in the Near East sometime in the distant past.

So imagine my surprise when I learned that Coatlicue, the Aztec (okay, Mexica) Earth mother, has her claws wrapped around a root of the World Tree.

As it turns out, the idea of an *axis mundi* is common to countless belief systems around the world. Totem poles carved by Native American tribes in the Pacific Northwest are another form. So is Mount Fuji to the Japanese. So are the Black Hills in South Dakota to the Sioux.

Maybe 9/11 was so horrifying to Americans in part because two of our iconic *axes mundi* – the twin towers of the World Trade Center – fell before our eyes.

Which provides a perfect segue to my final point of this introduction.

A word about Good vs. Evil

The Pipe Woman Chronicles are urban fantasy – a subdivision, if you will, of the broader genre called fantasy – and one of fantasy's hallmarks, besides the presence of magic, is the struggle between Good and Evil. You see this especially in epic fantasy: the hero is usually pure of heart, despite his or her self-doubts, and finds him- or herself pitted against a being of Pure Evil. Think the devil, or Bram Stoker's Dracula, or Sauron in *Lord of the Rings*. We as readers might get an origin story for the world, but we never get inside the monster's head to find out what's going on up there. He might as well have a big ol' neon sign plastered across his forehead: "EVIL INCARNATE!" It's the hero's job, then, to stop Mr. Pure Evil from carrying out his nefarious plans.

I deliberately did not create a being of Pure Evil in any of the *Pipe Woman Chronicles* books. And I had good reasons for it.

For one thing, in terms of story mechanics, it's a lazy way out. You don't have to come up with any motivation for your bad guy; he's evil because he's evil. If you look deeply into a bad guy's psyche – if you try to see him as a real person instead of a convenient punching bag – the first thing you'll realize is that the bad guy doesn't really think he's bad. He's just misunderstood. Thwarted at every turn. If only people would take the time to understand him, they'd help him – but they never do. Or they think he's crazy – which he might actually be, but even the criminally insane have internal reasons for what they do.

Stephen R. Donaldson plays with this idea in his *Chronicles of Thomas Covenant the Unbeliever*. (You knew I had to work in a Donaldson reference, didn't you? Of course you did.) Among Donaldson's creations are the Ravers, three beings of utter malice who serve Lord Foul in his bid to take over the Land. But the Ravers don't see themselves as bad guys, and the Sanskrit words they use to refer to themselves reflect that. Herem calls himself *turiya*, which is the fourth stage of consciousness, beyond thought and will. Jehannum calls himself *moksha*, or freedom from the world of ordinary experience. And Sheol calls himself *samadhi*, which is the highest meditative state one can reach. In other words, these guys all believe themselves to be operating on a higher spiritual plane than mere mortals. How could anything they do be evil? They're clearly above all that.

In short, the Ravers could have been just cookie-cutter monsters recruited by Foul to do his bidding – but they're not. In fact, they don't think they're evil at all.

The other reason I didn't stick a stock Evil Character in any of the *Pipe Woman Chronicles* is that I felt it wouldn't be true to the source material.

The first chroniclers of newly-discovered peoples filtered what they learned through their own cultural biases, and then sifted these peoples' legends and myths through that filter when they wrote them down. It wasn't deliberate; it's just the way humans operate. When we run across a new thing, we compare it to a sort of similar thing we already know about, and classify it as being like the thing we already knew.

But that's a dangerous assumption to make; the new thing is likely not that similar to our familiar thing at all. Yet that's what many of the early chroniclers of indigenous belief systems inadvertently did. And because most of the chroniclers were Christian, Christian beliefs often ended up overlaid on top of the original myths. Christianity puts a lot of stock in the dichotomy of Good vs. Evil, and so the non-Western myths we read today are often cast in that mold. But the Good/Evil dichotomy may not have been in the indigenous myths to start with; instead, the stories may have been meant to emphasize the importance of keeping the world *in balance*.

I'm reminded of the Slavic legend of Perun and Veles, which comes up in the *Pipe Woman's Legacy* books. Perun is the Slavic thunder god; Veles oversees Nav, the underworld. At certain times of the year, Veles picks a fight with Perun so that Perun will throw thunderbolts at Him. Then the rains come and the plants grow. A Christian reading of the myth might call Veles evil – He runs the underworld, after all, and He hassles Perun by stealing His stuff so that Perun will chase Him and cause violent weather in our world. But Veles is simply doing His job, keeping the world in balance. After all, if there is no rain, the crops will die and the people will starve. But too much rain might cause flooding. So it's Perun's job to make sure rainy days are balanced with fine days. That's neither Good nor Evil. That's just how things are.

One last thing

I've deliberately left out three of the deities that show up in my books: Jehovah, Jesus, and Lucifer. Most Western readers have a firm enough grasp on Them that I didn't think I needed to include Them in this guide. However, I'm happy to entertain arguments to the contrary. If you'd like me to reconsider, feel free to drop me a note at lynne.cantwell@hearth-myth.com.

Creators

Ah, humans. Are they not ingenious? I am proud of them.

Jehovah, *Annealed*

One thing about creation myths: Every religion's got one.

People who study myths have created several systems for classifying creation myths. Here's one typical system, from Wikipedia:

- *Ex nihilo*, or from nothing.

- Creation from chaos. This might be considered a variation on the *ex nihilo* type, where the raw materials of creation start out as a formless void. An example would be the first creation story in Genesis: "In the beginning, God created the heaven and the earth." In both of these types, the creative force is often male.

- <u>Earth diver</u>. In an Ojibwe creation story, Nanabozho finds Himself adrift on a raft in a vast sea. He sends various animals to dive far below the raft to find a grain of soil or sand. At last, the muskrat succeeds, and the single grain of soil he retrieves expands to become Turtle Island – otherwise known as North America.

- <u>Emergence</u>. A number of Southwestern tribes – among them, the Pueblo and the Aztec – believe humanity is making progress upward from one world to the next. Oftentimes the people are led up to the new world through a hole in the sky. A female deity, often Grandmother Spider or Spider Woman, is the prime mover in these tales.

- <u>World parents</u>. These myths involve both a male and female deity – Father Sky and Mother Earth, if you will – who join together to create the world and everything on it. In some myths, the humans then have to figure out a way to prop up Father Sky so they have room for themselves in between Him and Mother Earth.

- <u>Cosmic egg</u>. One example would be the Orphic Egg of Greek mythology, which came with a serpent wrapped around it. The hermaphroditic deity that hatched from this egg then created the other gods and goddesses.

As you can see from this less-than-exhaustive list, the deity who makes the heaven and the earth isn't always male. In addition, there are gods and goddesses who create culture for Their people by teaching them survival skills. The *Pipe Woman Chronicles* books feature both world creators and culture creators.

White Buffalo Calf Pipe Woman

*Lakota – Naomi Witherspoon Curtis – **Seized***

I'm putting White Buffalo Calf Pipe Woman first because She is the spirit who sets the story in motion. (I'm told the Lakota simply call her White Buffalo Woman, which is a much smaller mouthful. Had I known that, Naomi and the gang would have referred to her by name a whole lot more often!)

In the sweat lodge scene in *Seized*, the Ute shaman Looks Far Guzmán recounts the legend of White Buffalo Calf Pipe Woman. I'm going to let him do the honors here.

"This is not a Ute legend," he said at the outset. "It's Sioux. It has almost become a pan-Indian legend over the years, though, along with many other legends and practices that were once theirs only. Some of the Sioux aren't too happy about the way the whites have co-opted their culture, although their nation isn't the only one to be treated so. Sometimes it seems as if the whites think of us Indians as all one happy family, with the same religion and the same way of life – as if all Indians lived in tepees and built totem poles.

"Anyway, this is how I heard it…

"Two braves were out hunting one day, without much luck. This was not good – their tribe was very hungry. Suddenly they spied something in the distance. As it came nearer, they realized it was a beautiful Indian maiden, dressed all in white buckskin and floating instead of walking…"

"One of the young men told his friend, 'That beautiful maiden is for me! I'm going to go and get her!' The friend cautioned him, saying he thought the woman was sacred. But the first young man laughed him off. Well, when he went to touch the woman, lightning came out of nowhere and struck him, so that nothing but ash and bits of bone were left.

"The woman told the second young man that She was from the buffalo nation, and She had something holy to give to his people. She told him to go back to camp and tell the people there to prepare for Her arrival. They were to put up a medicine lodge with twenty-eight poles and await Her coming.

"All was in readiness when the woman arrived, four days later. She brought them the sacred pipe of their nation and taught them how to use it. She taught them the seven sacred ceremonies in which to use the pipe. She taught the women how to make a hearth fire, and how to cook food in a buffalo paunch by dropping a hot stone into it. She taught the tribe everything it needed to know to survive and to honor the spirits in the proper way.

"When She had taught them everything, She told their chief that She was the four ages of creation, and that She would return at the end of every age. Then She walked off, into the setting sun. As the people watched Her go, they saw Her roll over and turn into a black buffalo; then She rolled over again, and turned into a brown buffalo; then She rolled over a third time, and turned into a red buffalo; and the fourth time She rolled over, she turned into a white buffalo calf – the most sacred animal of the Sioux."

One of the seven sacred ceremonies White Buffalo Woman taught Her people was the *hunkpapa* ceremony, in which a member of the tribe adopts an adult who isn't a blood relation. I described my version of a *hunkpapa* ceremony in a scene in *Annealed*.

Bear Mother

Tlingit – Sandy Hanlon (mother of Rafe Orloff) – **Dragon's Web**

From the Great Plains, we travel north to the Pacific Northwest for the Tlingit myth of Bear Mother. This version comes from *Heroes and Heroines in Tlingit-Haida Legend* by Mary Beck.

The tale begins on a summer's day, as a tribal princess and three of her friends go berry-picking. The girls are supposed to sing as they tramp through the woods, to warn away any bears. But the princess gets tired of singing and begins chattering about her suitors and so on. While thus distracted, she slips on a pile of bear dung and falls. "Those stupid, dirty bears!" she cries. "Why don't they watch where they do their messes?"

Well, a Bear prince heard her, and decided to teach her a lesson. Besides, she was cute. So he disguised himself as a human and, when the princess became separated from her friends, he stepped out of the woods and offered to take her home. Of course, he had no intention of doing so. Instead, he took her to his own home, where he introduced the princess to his parents as his bride.

The young princess settled into her new home, with nary a thought to her own family. She even bore her husband two sons. But one night, three years after coming to live with the Bears, she awoke in the middle of the night to find a grizzly sleeping next to her. It was her husband, of course, and when she cried out, he awoke and confessed everything. But he refused to let her go home.

All this time, her family had been searching for her. Some members of the tribe believed the princess was dead, but her family never gave up hope.

At last, her youngest brother decided to take his dog and a hunting party and go looking for her. His brothers laughed at him – but he succeeded where they had not. He and his dog discovered the hidden cave where the Bear prince had been living with his sister. The Bear knew his brother-in-law would kill him, so he didn't fight; instead, he turned his little cubs into humans and told them, "Go with your mother. You will become the greatest of hunters." He sang his own funeral dirge. And then he allowed the princess's brother to kill him with an arrow shot.

The princess wept for her husband, but took her children home. And as the children grew, they taught their superior hunting skills to the tribe.

So although Bear Mother's story is a cautionary tale about following tribal protocol, it also explains why it's important for people to learn from those outside their own tribe – because that way, everyone has a better chance of surviving.

Spider Woman

*Navajo – Webb Curtis – **Spider's Lifeline***

Spider Woman is the goddess who taught the Navajo how to weave. But Her roots are with the Anasazi, the ancestors of the Pueblo Indians, and their Grandmother Spider. The Pueblo consider Grandmother Spider a creatrix; it was She who created them from clay, and it was also She who led them to the Fourth World, where we live now.

In *Grandmothers of the Light*, Paula Gunn Allen, who is Laguna Pueblo, said the creation goddess of her people is also known as Thought Woman: "Grandmother Spider, Thought Woman, thought the earth, the sky, the galaxy, and all that is into being, and as she thinks, so are we."

While the Navajos' Spider Woman did not create Her people, She was instrumental in helping them to survive. In one myth, She allows them to learn how to get rid of all the monsters that were living in the world when they arrived.

She also taught the Navajo how to weave on a loom – including how to weave in a small flaw: a spirit line or lifeline that extends a row of the interior design to one edge of the weaving. The weaver puts it there to keep his or her energy from being trapped in the rug. I thought it fitting that Spider Woman would be weaving a rug for Webb when he runs into Her, somewhere in New Mexico, in *Spider's Lifeline.*

Coatlicue

Aztec/Mexica – Jack Rivers – **Fissured**

Now we head south to Mexico and the Aztec (or more properly, the Mexica) mother goddess, Coatlicue.

You have to give the Aztecs props for one thing: They don't have much in the way of cuddly deities. Two serpents, facing each other and made of blood, form Coatlicue's head. Her skirt, too, is made of serpents, and She wears a necklace of human skulls, hearts and hands. Her taloned feet clutch a root of the Aztec world tree.

Coatlicue was a sacrificial mother figure: the goddess who birthed, or rebirthed, Huitzilopochtli, the god who led the Aztec people from their original homeland of Aztlán to Mexico. As Coatlicue was sweeping out a temple at Coatepec in Mexico, She caught a ball of feathers and tucked it inside Her shirt. When She was done sweeping, the feathers had disappeared, and She realized they had impregnated Her. Her other children – four hundred sons and a daughter – were so upset with Their mother that They plotted to kill Her. But when They cut off Coatlicue's head, Huitzilapochtli sprang from Her body, dismembered His sister, and killed nearly all of His brothers.

Experts speculate this tale of the rebirth of Huitzilapochtli may relate to the ascendance of a new, very human leader of the Aztecs who may have been seen as the second coming of the god. But it also shows Coatlicue as a figure in the spirit of the Hindu goddess Kali – both creator and destroyer. Just like the Earth itself.

A much later legend has followers of the fifth king of the Aztecs, Moctezuma, traveling to find Aztlán. Moctezuma heard that Coatlicue was still alive there, and sent his ambassadors with gifts for Her. When the travelers arrived, they learned Coatlicue had been crying day and night for Huitzilapochtli. It seems that when He left Aztlán for his people's new homeland, He had promised His mother that He would return to Her someday. The ambassadors had the sad duty of telling Coatlicue that Her son had been dead for many, many years.

Cerridwen

*Celtic (Welsh) – Sage Curtis – **Firebird's Snare***

Cerridwen (whose name is often spelled with only one "r") was a legendary Welsh figure whose tale appears in the *Mabinogion*. She was the mother of two children, a beautiful daughter named Creirwy and a hideous son named Morfran (or, sometimes, Afagddu). She wanted Her son to be successful, as all mothers do, so she set Her cauldron bubbling with a stew that was meant to give Morfran great wisdom and a gift for poetry. But only the first three drops of the concoction were any good.

The mess had to cook for a year and a day. Cerridwen had other stuff to do, so She set a boy named Gwion Bach to the job of stirring the cauldron. But the stew bubbled up and three drops splattered on Gwion's thumb. He stuck his burned thumb in his mouth – and hey presto, he acquired all the knowledge Cerridwen had meant for Her son.

Cerridwen, as you might expect, was not pleased. So Gwion fled, and used his newfound knowledge to change his shape in order to fool Cerridwen. But She was not fooled at all. When Gwion changed into a hare, She became a greyhound; when he became a fish, She shifted to an otter; when he shifted to a bird, She became a hawk. Finally, he changed himself into a grain of corn and hid in a pile of the stuff. But She found him and ate him – and was impregnated. Furious, She resolved to kill him at birth, but couldn't do it. Instead, She set him adrift in the ocean. A Welsh king rescued him, and the child grew into the great Welsh poet Taliesin.

Frigga

Norse – none – **Tapped**

Frigga is the Anglicized form of the name of the Norse goddess Frigg. It's possible Frigg and Freya were once the same goddess, although the two are understood today to be different deities entirely. Freya is associated with love, lust, war, and death. But Frigga is the wife of Odin, the Allfather of the Norse pantheon. In Her own right, She is the goddess of marriage, childbirth, and household management – including weaving and spinning. She and Odin had two sons, Baldur and Hodor. Frigga also had the gift of foreknowledge, although it wasn't quite enough to save one of Her sons from killing the other. Although really, that was Loki's fault.

Oh, let's save that story for later in the book.

Ingun

Norse – Ingrid Ingunnardottir – **Turtle's Weir**

References to this early Norse goddess are difficult to come by. In *Norse Mythology: A Guide to Gods, Heroes, Rituals, and Beliefs*, John Lindow mentions Ingun in connection with Frey; Ingunar-Frey, he says, was Frey's title in the *Great Saga of St. Olaf*. Lindow goes on to quote a couple of scholars, one of whom believed Ingun was the Earth, and another of whom argued that She was a fertility goddess. Another source I found translated Frey as, simply, Lord. Putting the two together would make Ingunar-Frey "the Lord of the Earth" – which tallies with the idea of Ingun as Frey's consort. Yet another source suggested She may have been Frey's mother, which sounds vaguely incestuous until you consider that ancient Irish kings were expected to mate with the land, either literally or figuratively, and it's not beyond the realm of possibility that Norse rulers would have had to do the same.

In any case, it appears Ingun's place in the Norse pantheon was subsumed by another, more popular goddess. An online mythology dictionary calls Her "an aspect of Freya as a fertility-goddess," which seems plausible to me. Another online source calls her "the Progenitrix, Birthgiver and Devourer" – titles attributable to a whole host of Earth goddesses.

I stitched all of these ideas together to create my version of Ingun: a sexy creatrix/destroyer who feels that Her followers were stolen from Her, and She would like them back, thank you very much.

Pele

Hawaiian – Nick Higoshi – **Annealed**

Pele's mythological cycle explains, in part, the formation of the Hawaiian islands. I found Her story in *Hawaiian Mythology* by Martha Beckwith.

As Beckwith tells it, Pele came from a land far away from Hawaii. She was beautiful, "with a back straight as a cliff and breasts rounded like the moon," and with a fiery nature, as well. There are a number of versions of the legend – but in many of them, the goddess visits each of the Hawaiian islands in turn, digging a pit on each one as She looks for a new home. She ends up at last on the Big Island of Hawaii, where She finds Kilauea, a volcano that's big enough for Her family and Her fire.

When I visited Hawaii, I learned that each of the islands had started life as an underwater volcano. Over time, lava from the eruptions built up, so that eventually the pile of lava was higher than sea level. Moreover, just as in the story of Pele's journey, the northwestern islands formed first, with the undersea volcanic activity progressing south and east to form new islands along the way.

And it's still going on. There's a seamount, or submerged peak, called Lo'ihi, about twenty miles off the southeast coast of the Big Island. The caldera is about three miles in diameter, and deep-sea cameras have captured images of lava flows that have probably formed within the past hundred years. Studies indicate Lo'ihi is tapping the same magma supply as the Mauna Loa and Kilauea volcanoes on the Big Island.

In 1996, after thousands of minor earthquakes had shaken the area, teams of scientists went underwater to study what was going on. They found that the summit of Lo'ihi had collapsed and formed a new pit crater, which has been dubbed Pele's Pit. Maybe the fire goddess is still looking for the perfect volcanic home for Her family, after all.

Gaia

*Neopagan/Classical (Greek) – Sue Killeen -- **Crosswind***

For the ancient Greeks, Gaia was the original Earth mother. Hesiod, in his *Theogony*, depicted Her as rising from Chaos to create Olympus, thereafter the home of the gods. She then created Uranus, or the sky, and Pontus, the sea. And She gave birth to the Titans, the heavenly gods, and the Giants – sometimes without having to consort with anybody.

I lean more toward the modern Neopagan interpretation of Her. So in the *Pipe Woman Chronicles*, Gaia is literally the mother of the Earth. Oberon Zell's statue is what I had in mind when I created the character of Gaia for my books: a woman whose hair and skin are rich with flora and fauna, and whose belly is swollen with an Earth that's forever being born anew.

The Rainbow Serpent

Australian Aboriginal – Merindah O'Connor – **Annealed**

This Australian aboriginal spirit – or more accurately, spirits – provide us with a segue from female to male creators, because Rainbow Serpents come in both kinds.

But first, I'd like to talk about the Dreamtime.

In the Judeo-Christian creation timeline, God created the heaven and the earth at some indeterminate time in the past – the key phrase being "in the past." God still exists, putting His hand in here and there to answer prayers (in most Judeo-Christian traditions) or not (in the Deist and clockwork-universe traditions), but the process of creating everything took Him six days. Then He took a day off, and then He made Adam and Eve. After that, He spoke to an occasional prophet. Later on, He sent humanity His own Son. But all of that stuff in the Bible happened a really long time ago (except for the Book of Revelation, which I am not going to get into).

So it's natural for those of us who grew up as Westerners to look at other peoples' mythologies and believe that they, too, happened in some misty past. But when you're talking about Aboriginal people in Australia, or Native Americans, or other indigenous peoples around the world, that attitude is a mistake. They're still living in sacred time. For them, the Dreamtime is happening right now.

It's admittedly a tough concept for Westerners. Maybe it will help to put it in terms familiar to readers of speculative fiction: you could describe the Dreamtime as existing in a sort of parallel universe to ours, where time flows differently. You could step over into this place if you knew how, and some people do. Meditation, ritual dance, drumming, and mind-altering substances have all been used to step across.

Anyway, the Rainbow Serpents exist in the Dreamtime. They are tied to water and, by extension, to fertility, water being critical to life in arid lands. In some myths, They create humans; in others, They destroy them (by sending floodwaters, for instance). For some Aboriginal people, the Rainbow Serpent is female, the mother of creation; for others, the Rainbow Serpent is male, the being that transforms the land.

Researchers in Australia have found rock art depictions of Rainbow Serpents that date back six thousand years – which would make the Rainbow Serpent the oldest continuous religious tradition in the world.

Blood Clot Boy

Ute – Looks Far Guzmán – **Seized**

Legends of a boy born from a clot of blood are rife in Native American legend. I based my depiction of Blood Clot Boy on the

Southern Ute tale related in *American Indian Myths and Legends*, edited by Richard Erdoes and Alfonso Ortiz.

As the story begins, a poor, elderly couple are living in an isolated tent. Hunting has been bad and they are hungry. One day, the old man runs across some buffalo tracks and follows them. What he finds is a clot of blood, apparently left behind by the buffalo who made the tracks. So the old man scoops up the clot and takes it home, figuring he and his wife can at least have blood soup for dinner.

The wife puts the blood clot in the pot and sets it on the fire. Before long, the two of them hear a baby crying. They look in the pot, and sure enough, a baby boy has emerged from the clot of blood. So they take him out, clean him up, and decide to raise him.

It doesn't take long. Within three days, the boy is walking. The old man makes the boy some arrows so He can learn to shoot. Shortly thereafter, the kid starts bringing home game: first a mouse, then a rabbit, and so on. The day the boy brings down a deer, they all eat very well.

Each time the boy kills something, He sends His father out to find it. And it's the old man, not the old woman, who cooks everything the boy kills for them.

This goes on for a while. At last, Blood Clot Boy tells His parents that He will be gone on a big hunting trip overnight. Before He leaves, He instructs them to tie down their tent firmly and weight the edges with rocks. He tells them they will hear a big wind, but they should stay inside and not be afraid. They do as He says, and then go to sleep.

Around dawn, they awaken to the fiercest windstorm they've ever heard in their lives. But they stay inside the tent, as their son told them to do. The wind eventually stops, and when their son beckons them outside, they see their tent is surrounded by dead buffalo. Blood Clot Boy tells them He has to leave, but if they dry the buffalo meat and the hides, they will be set for a very long time. His parents are sorry to see Him go, of course, and they ask Him to come home someday.

Blood Clot Boy travels for several days before coming to a village. He asks the villagers there to help Him figure out which tribe He belongs to, and one old man says, judging by the power He senses in Blood Clot Boy, He must be of the Buffalo tribe.

These people, too, are starving. Blood Clot Boy marries the chief's daughter and provides His own wedding feast with the same wind-and-dead-buffalo trick He pulled for his parents. All is well for many years, until Blood Clot Boy's wife utters the word "calf." At that instant, the young man runs away, changing into a buffalo as He flees, and is never seen again.

The book doesn't state this, but I can't help thinking Blood Clot Boy is not simply providing for His people. Instead, I bet, He's teaching them how to provide for themselves. After all, He sends His father out to pick up the meat – so the older man then knows where game is plentiful. And He tells His parents how to preserve the bounty of buffalo meat and hides He has brought them. So like White Buffalo Calf Pipe Woman, Blood Clot Boy teaches His tribe how to survive.

Quetzalcoatl

*Aztec/Mexica – none – **Fissured***

Our one and only Feathered Serpent is evidently a bigger deal now than He was in the past, as Mesoamerican belief systems featured a number of avian serpents.

Quetzalcoatl's name comes from the Nahuatl, or Aztec language, words for the emerald green feathers of the quetzal bird and the rattlesnake. He is most often depicted as an anthromorphic figure with a bird's beak for a mouth and a feathered ruff.

The fates of Quetzalcoatl and Tezcatlipoca are tied in a number of myths. In one legend, the two are brothers whose parents, Tonacateuctli and Tonacacihuatl, tell Them to make the world. This sets the stage for a legendary battle that renews itself throughout history. Sometimes Quetzalcoatl wins; sometimes Tezcatlipoca does. In terms of this myth, we are now living in the fifth age and Tezcatlipoca is currently in charge – but Quetzalcoatl may make His triumphant return at any time.

For many years, scholars thought that when Hernán Cortéz arrived in Mexico in 1519, Emperor Moctezuma II believed the Spanish explorer to be Quetzalcoatl reborn and basically handed over his throne. More recent scholarship indicates that was probably wishful thinking as reported by Cortéz and his men; more likely it was Moctezuma's people themselves who overthrew him, creating political chaos that Cortéz simply took advantage of. Regardless, the arrival of Cortéz and other explorers was devastating for many aspects of Aztec life, including their religion.

Some Christian scholars have tried, over the years, to recast Quetzalcoatl as a Christian figure in disguise. Father Diego Durán, a Dominican friar who chronicled many Aztec myths just after the time of the conquistadores, believed Quetzalcoatl to be St. Thomas. Today, some Mormons reportedly believe He was Jesus Christ.

The winter solstice of 2012 was supposed to herald, among other things, the end of Tezcatlipoca's rule and the return of Quetzalcoatl. In other words, the bad guy was supposed to be hustled off the throne and replaced by the good guy. But don't forget: Christianity has often overlaid ancient myths with a Good-vs.-Evil dichotomy that wasn't originally there. Quetzalcoatl was a Trickster in His own right; He wasn't all good, any more than Tezcatlipoca was all bad. Perhaps in this case, as in many cases, we should be careful what we wish for, lest we get it.

Odin

*Norse – none – **Seized***

I admit I have not looked quite as deeply into Norse myth as I should have. Much of my knowledge of the pantheon stems from remembering what I learned in school, together with internet searches, the Marvel Universe movies, and, in this case, Neil Gaiman's depiction of Odin in his novel *American Gods*. I do intend to read the Elder Eddas someday, I swear it.

That *mea culpa* aside (it's the first of several, I assure you), I'll tell you what I understand of Odin. First, he's the Allfather – the head of the Norse pantheon – and Frigga is his wife. He rules Valhalla, the afterlife of warriors who have died in battle.

Odin has a long beard and only one eye; He surrendered the other eye to Mimir, the guardian of the well of wisdom among the roots of Yggdrasil, in exchange for a drink from the well. He rides Sleipnir – an eight-legged horse to which Loki gave birth while in the form of a mare – and is accompanied by two ravens, Huginn and Muninn. And He sometimes travels in disguise as an old man with a staff, wearing a broad-brimmed hat and a blue or black cloak – which is how Naomi first sees Him in a vision in *Seized*.

Well, actually, it might not have been Odin she saw. Let's just leave it at that.

Guardians

A few weeks earlier, a Lakota Sioux goddess had charged Joseph with being my Guardian. Why did I need a Guardian, you ask? Why, because She had chosen me to save the world.

Like they say on Facebook, it's complicated.

Naomi Witherspoon, *Fissured*

Guardian deities are tasked with protecting everything from creation, to legendary figures, to their own people.

I had fun tweaking this idea in the various books of the series, and even occasionally standing it on its head. Before the story in *Seized* even starts, Joseph believes he is destined to be the Guardian for White Buffalo Calf Pipe Woman's chosen one. As a modern, independent woman, Naomi has no patience for that sort of thing – particularly after Jack shows up in *Fissured*. And as the series progresses, Naomi protects Joseph as often as he protects her.

In the *Land, Sea, Sky* books, it's Morrigan who's charged with protecting Tess, while also teaching her how strong she can be.

And in the *Pipe Woman's Legacy* books, Rafe would be Sage's Guardian, except that she keeps having to rescue him from people and critters who are trying to kill him.

Not all of the entities in this chapter are deities, technically. But They have all been put in charge of guarding something, and that's how I thought of Them when I was writing about Them in my books.

Wolf Dreamer

Lakota – Andrew Sauvage – **Tapped**

Well, this is embarrassing.

When I started planning *Tapped*, I had a great fractalized photo of a wolf that I wanted to use on the cover. That meant I had to put a wolf in the story – and the wolf had to represent Naomi's father, Drew, because the plot of the book revolved around her going to South Dakota to find him. When I saw a reference to a Wolf Dreaming society among the Sioux, I thought I was home free.

But information on Wolf Dreamers proved to be elusive, both in print and online. I found some generalized information about Sioux dreaming societies, and some details on the other societies. But none on the Wolf Dreamers – except for one book that I found online via Google Books. It had a quote from an interview with a Wolf Dreamer, even. But it was unavailable or out of print or too expensive or something. Anyway, I didn't buy it.

Did I make a note of the title and author? Of course not. Have I been able to find it online now, four years later? Of course not.

So all I have to offer is this excerpt from *Tapped*, in which Drew and his brother Thom explain to Naomi and Shannon what a Wolf Dreamer is, and why Drew isn't one anymore.

"What's a wolf dream?" Shannon asked. "Is there something special about it?"

In reply, Drew walked across the room to the door with the shield on it. He yanked open the door and stepped back. I inhaled sharply. On the back of the door hung a wolf skin, the skull still in place. The blank eyes seemed to stare at us more menacingly than real eyes ever could.

Once I tore my eyes away from the wolf skin, I noticed other regalia stored in the tiny closet – an elaborately painted shield, a decorated spear, and what I assumed was a ceremonial costume.

"I am a Wolf Dreamer," Drew said. Then, bitterly, he added, "Or I was."

"I don't understand," Shannon said.

Thom took up the story. "Most Plains Indian tribes developed warrior societies during the buffalo years. There were many societies. Membership in some was based on a man's age, or on his ability to fight. But the dreaming societies were different. All you had to do to get into one of those was to have a dream about a particular animal, and do the things the spirit animal told you to do in your dream."

"I was sixteen when I dreamed of Wolf the first time," Drew said, his eyes far away.

"We were living in Lafayette at the time," Thom explained, "nowhere near the tribe. There was no one Drew could turn to for the help he needed to understand his vision."

"In the days of the buffalo," said Drew, "the Wolf Dreamer would go apart from the hunting party and cry for a vision from Wolf. Wolf would tell the Dreamer where the buffalo were grazing and how best to kill them, so that the tribe would survive the winter." He dropped his head. "But there are no buffalo roaming the plains now. I was a Wolf

Dreamer without a purpose." He lifted his eyes to me. "So I joined the Army."

"He thought they could use his tracking skills," Thom said. "And he advanced pretty fast, too."

"I'd made it to staff sergeant by the time my unit was deployed in 'Nam," Drew said. "We were among the last units to be pulled out of Saigon. Our mission was to get the American civilians in Saigon out safely, before the city fell to the Viet Cong.

"One night, I dreamed of a pack of wolves running through the streets of Saigon. They stopped in front of a riverfront warehouse near our position and bayed. I knew what it meant – the Viet Cong were hunkered down inside that warehouse, waiting to attack. The next day, I pleaded with my C.O. to let me take my men there and clean it out. But he wouldn't agree to it. He said our job was to get the civilians out, and that's what we were going to do.

"That afternoon, as we were loading the last of the civilians onto a helicopter, the V.C. opened fire on us. The civilians all got out okay, but everybody in my unit was killed. Everybody except me."

"That's when you lost your arm," I said softly.

His voice dropped to a whisper. "I could have saved them all. I could have disobeyed orders. But I didn't, and they all died. Because I did what I was told. Because I ignored Wolf."

And that's all I can tell you about Wolf Dreamers. Sorry about that.

Morrigan

Celtic (Irish) – Tess Showalter – **Crosswind**

I'm on firmer ground here.

Three was a sacred number for the ancient Celts, so it shouldn't be surprising that some of their deities are sort of three-in-one. The Morrigan is one of these.

Accounts vary as to which three goddesses make up Her trinity. Badb (goddess of battle) and Macha (goddess of war and horses) are usually two of them, with the third sometimes being Anand (which may or may not be another name for Morrigan), sometimes Nemain (who may or may not be Badb), and sometimes Morrigan Herself. And sometimes Morrigan is considered an individual, independent goddess. It's confusing, to say the least.

In any case, the Morrigan is considered a dark, scary figure today – the Irish goddess of war, accompanied by Her crows. One of Her earliest appearances in Irish mythology is in the Ulster cycle, in which She foretells the death of the hero

Cuchulainn. Some time afterward, he sees Her as a hag, washing his bloody armor in a ford. He knows it's a bad omen, and he's right; he dies in battle later that day.

But as Sue tells Tess in *Crosswind*, Morrigan is also a goddess of sovereignty – a goddess of the land. Her connection to war may simply be a facet of Her duty to protect the king. Some myths support this view. In addition, She is associated with cattle, which you have to admit are pretty earthy. And in County Meath, I've heard, there's a pair of hills called the "two breasts of the Morrigan," similar to the Paps of Anu in County Kerry. You can't get much earthier than having your boobs included in the landscape.

Some have attempted to conflate the Morrigan with Morgan le Fay in the King Arthur tales. But linguists say their names spring from different root words: Morgan comes from a Welsh root meaning "the sea," while Morrigan's root is Irish and means either "terror" or "greatness." Either way, I wouldn't cross Her.

Thor

Norse – Kurt Lange – **Fissured**

Ah, yes, my next *mea culpa*. As I explained when I talked about Odin, most of my knowledge of Norse mythology comes from what little I learned in school, together with internet searches and the "Avengers" movies.

So I can tell you that Thor is a big, red-haired guy who wields a hammer named Mjollnir that nobody but He can lift. He is the god of thunder and lightning, but He is also associated with oak trees and the protection of humankind. His father is Odin; his mother is not Frigga, but Jord – also known as Earth.

In some accounts, Thor is married to Sif (which was inconvenient enough for Marvel that they made Sif just another warrior and had Thor fall in love with an American woman). The Thor-Sif pairing would make sense if you thought of Thor as a sky god and Sif an earth goddess. And maybe that's who They were, back in the misty Norse past.

In the *Pipe Woman Chronicles*, Thor is mostly tasked with keeping Loki out of trouble – which works about as well as you'd expect.

Perun

Slavic – Paul Orloff – **Dragon's Web**

Perun might be considered the Slavic pantheon's Thor. He, too, is a red-haired god of thunder. His ultimate weapon is a battle-ax instead of a hammer, and He also carries a bow from which He shoots lightning bolts.

There, the similarities stop. For Perun is generally thought to be the highest god in the Slavic pantheon, even though He isn't their creator god; that honor falls to Rod.

Oak trees were considered sacred to the Slavs – the Slavic world tree is an oak – and shrines to Perun were often located under particularly large and venerable specimens, with His image carved into the living tree. His shrines were also built atop mountains or hills. When Vladimir the Great assumed the throne in Kiev in 980, he had five statues of Slavic gods erected there; chief among them was Perun, with a silver head and golden mustaches.

Perun can get cranky. He gets the blame for all sorts of natural calamities, including earthquakes and violent storms. In the Introduction, I alluded to the cyclical battle between Perun and Veles, the Slavic god of the underworld. Veles starts things off by slithering up the trunk of the World Tree in His serpent shape, and stealing something Perun values – His cattle, His wife, or one of His offspring. Perun then gets mad and aims lightning bolts at Veles. The underworld god runs and hides, transforming Himself into trees, animals, or people. At last, Perun kills Him, and what remains of Veles turns into rain. Never fear, though – Veles sheds His old skin and generates a new one, and the cycle begins again.

The *Encyclopedia Britannica* claims Perun was Christianized into St. Elijah the Thunderer, and His/their feast day is July 20.

While going through my mother's things after she died, I found a little booklet of Czech song lyrics that were handed out by a tavern in Chicago sometime during World War II. A number of the songs are drinking songs, as you might expect, but one of them calls on Perun to help the Czechs save their homeland from the Nazis. So even in 1940s America, Czechs knew who to call when the going got tough.

Diana

Classical (Roman) – Antonia Greco – **Gravid**

Diana is the Roman goddess of the hunt. She is also associated with the moon and with childbirth, and Her counterpart in the Greek pantheon is Artemis. She wears a short tunic and boots – practical attire for hunting – and carries a bow and arrows. A deer or hunting dogs often accompany Her. Her twin brother is Apollo, the god of the sun.

Diana is an appealing deity, even today. A branch of Wicca is named for Her. But in connection with the *Pipe Woman Chronicles*, perhaps the most interesting thing about Diana is Her association with stregheria. According to Raven Grimassi's website on the subject, stregheria was the Old Religion of Italy, with roots in an ancient Etruscan religion. At one time, its traditions were passed down within families, presumably to hide its existence from the Catholic Church, but that is no longer the case; today, anybody can join. Adherents of stregheria worship Diana as well as Rex Nemorensis, the priest of Her temple at Aricia.

Oya

Yoruba – Adio Ogwu – **Annealed**

At one point early in *Seized*, White Buffalo Calf Pipe Woman tells Naomi that nobody expects her to bring humanity around to lovingkindness all by herself. "Others have been empowered as well, in other parts of the world," the goddess tells her.

Naomi gets to meet a few of these others in the big mediation scene in *Annealed*. One of them is Adio Ogwu, a Nigerian woman who has been working with the Yoruba orisha (or deity) named Oya. Before the mediation starts, Adio chats briefly with Naomi and White Buffalo Calf Pipe Woman, who acknowledges that She is a sister goddess to one of Oya's aspects, Red Buffalo Woman.

Oya is the orisha of the winds of change, and Red Buffalo Woman's appearance certainly heralds a change for Chief of Hunters in this myth from *The Hero with an African Face* by Clyde W. Ford.

Chief of Hunters perches himself high in a tree, looking for game. He stays there all night with no luck. But as dawn breaks, a buffalo cow comes down the path below him. She looks right and left, and then begins to remove Her hide. When She is done, She is transformed into a beautiful woman, and Chief of Hunters decides he must have Her for a wife.

The woman hides Her skin, and heads off to the market with a load of locust beans She clearly intends to sell. Once She is out of sight, Chief of Hunters retrieves Her skin and stashes it at his own home. Then he goes to the market and convinces the woman to follow him home so he can pay Her for the beans he has bought from Her. As night falls, She makes Her way back to the place where She'd hidden Her skin, discovers it's gone, and realizes Chief of Hunters must have it. When She returns to his house and demands Her skin, he demands that She marry him. She agrees, on the condition that he never tell anyone where he found Her or what he took from Her.

Buffalo Woman is not his only wife — and Chief of Hunters' other wives are jealous of this red-haired stranger. So one night, they get Chief of Hunters drunk, and of course, he spills the beans.

The next day, the wives use the information to taunt Buffalo Woman. She realizes her time in that household is over — She can tone down Her wild nature to live in the wives' civilized society, and has, but the wives will never fully accept Her. It should be Chief of Hunters' job to mediate this dispute, but he has gone off to his farm for the day. So

Buffalo Woman sends Her children out to play, then retrieves Her skin and puts it on. Then She chases down Chief of Hunters' other wives and kills them.

Next, She finds Her children. They are frightened by Her appearance, but She breaks off a piece of Her horn and tells them to use it to call on Her – using Her real name, Oya – if they ever need Her help or protection.

Then She tracks down Chief of Hunters. As soon as he sees Her, he knows he's doomed. But he saves his own skin by praising Her and reminding Her of his kindness. She relents, and tells him that he, too, may call on Her if he ever needs Her.

So things changed in a hurry for Chief of Hunters. Due to his foolish behavior, he has lost much. But he gained the protection of Oya in the end. Perhaps he will be wiser from now on.

The Goddess of the Trees

Neopagan – Kalindra, High Priestess of the Grove of the Divine Spark –

Gravid

You caught me. Of all of the gods and goddesses in the ten books of the *Pipe Woman Chronicles*, the Goddess of the Trees is the only one I made up.

She lives in a magical grove of trees in a park in Boulder, Colorado, and Her high priestess contacts Naomi as events unfold in *Gravid*.

But don't be too hard on me; my fake tree goddess isn't unique. After all, the Greeks had their dryads and hamadryads; the Japanese, their kodama; and the Slavs, their leshy, one-eyed spirits that would lead young women into the woods for nefarious purposes.

And Tolkien invented Ents. So there.

Tricksters

> Just what I needed – another Trickster in my life.
>
> Sage Curtis, *Firebird's Snare*

When I was planning the *Pipe Woman Chronicles* books, it seemed like I was crossing paths with a Trickster every time I turned around. By the time I got to the *Legacy* books, things had gotten pretty chaotic – and then my editors, Susan Strayer and Kat Milyko, began lobbying for the addition of a kappa. They proceeded to explain that a kappa was a Japanese water demon. "And they're Tricksters!" Susan said, as if that settled it. Although it might have been Kat who said it. Anyway, it worked. Enkou was in. Clearly, they know me too well.

In mythology, Tricksters play several roles – sometimes all at once. They can be creators, as we'll see when we get to Raven; They can be the force of chaos, whose unpredictable and sometimes malicious behavior pushes both gods and humans to grow in unexpected ways; and They can be the goofball Everyman, to whom bad things happen so people can be taught how to avoid them.

As a writer, I find Tricksters a lot of fun to work with. They come up with stuff I never could have invented on my own. That whole elaborate prank on Jack toward the end of *Fissured*? I had nothing to do with it – it was all Joseph and Loki. As soon as Loki said to Joseph, "Have I ever told you about the time I shapechanged into a mare?" I realized my job for the next fifteen pages was simply to get out of their way.

Coyote

Ute – Joseph Curtis – **Seized**

Ah, Coyote. How can one god get into so much trouble?

Tales of Coyote abound in Native American mythologies, particularly those of the Plains and the Southwestern United States. In many of the tales, He is not a nice guy; instead, He's trying to steal something, or trick someone out of something, or trick a woman into having sex with Him. And he'll do virtually anything to get what He wants – including, of course, shapeshifting.

Ute Tales by Anne M. Smith includes a whole bunch of stories that feature Coyote in, shall we say, inappropriate situations. In one kind of mean-spirited tale, He steals a Bear's baby from its papoose, roasts it over a fire, convinces the Bear to eat it, and then harasses her for eating her own child.

The Jicarilla Apache have a less harrowing tale about Coyote that may sound familiar to people who remember the folktales of Uncle Remus. And who knows? The author of the Uncle Remus books, Joel Chandler Harris, may have lifted this story from Native American lore to start with.

I found this version at the following site: http://enargea.org/tales/Jicarilla/Pitch_Baby.html.

Coyote had a wife and children, but He was too lazy to plant His own corn patch. As a result, He and his family were hungry, so He went down to the people's corn patch and stole some of their corn. He waited until after midnight to go, because He knew everyone would be asleep then. And it worked – He didn't get caught. So He did it again. And again.

The people noticed their corn disappearing, of course, and they saw tracks in the patch that looked a bit like dog tracks. That made them suspect Coyote. So they set a trap for Him. They went into the forest and collected pine pitch and oak sap, and fashioned themselves a pitch baby – a little human-looking figure made out of sticky sap. They stood up their pitch baby on the path where they'd seen the footprints, and went to sleep.

Sure enough, under cover of darkness, Coyote strolled toward the corn patch for another round of thievery. He noticed the little figure on the path and stopped, thinking maybe He had been found out. He sidled up to the figure and said, "What are you doing here?"

No response.

"Are you lost?"

No response again. After a few more rounds of the silent treatment, Coyote got angry and slapped the figure – and His hand stuck fast.

Angrier than ever, He slapped it with His other hand – and that hand got stuck, too. Then He kicked it, and His foot stuck. Same with His other foot.

Then He pleaded with His silent captor: "My poor children are waiting for Me at home!" But of course there was no response from the pitch baby. At last, in fury, Coyote tried to bite the creature. Now not only was His mouth stuck, but He also couldn't talk.

And that's how the people found Him in the morning. They put a rope around His neck, pulled Him free of the trap, and dragged Him to face the tribal chief.

Coyote told the chief He hadn't been there to steal corn. No, certainly not. He'd been on another errand entirely, and had simply run into this thing in the dark. But the chief didn't buy it. He told Coyote the people had seen His tracks at the corn patch many times. And he warned Coyote not to come back, because next time no one would help Him get free of the pitch baby.

Empty-handed, Coyote headed home. He was still covered in pitch, and everything stuck to it. So when His wife saw Him, she yelled at Him for finding food and eating it all Himself without sharing any with His family.

And all because Coyote was too lazy to plant His own corn.

Nanabush (Nanabozho)

Ojibwe – Darrell Warren – **Crosswind**

Nanabozho, the Everyman god of the Anishinaabe, is a kinder, gentler Trickster than Coyote.

Anishinaabe is the classification for the languages spoken by tribes over a vast area of the upper Midwest of the US and Canada – Ojibwe (Chippewa), Odawa (Ottawa), Potawatomi, Algonquin, and Menominee among them. The dialects differ, and it all started out as oral myth anyway, so Nanabozho's name can be spelled a bunch of different ways. And you probably know

Him by a completely different name: Hiawatha. That's right – Henry Wadsworth Longfellow based his 19th-century epic poem on the tales of Nanabozho.

So why the name change? The real Hiawatha was a founding member of the League of the Iroquois, an unrelated tribal group whose lands lay in New York and Pennsylvania. But Henry Rowe Schoolcraft, an ethnographer and Indian agent, conflated the two names in his work, and Longfellow decided he liked the name Hiawatha better.

Anyway, Nanabozho was one of four sons of Winonah, a human woman, and Ae-pungishimook, the spirit of the West Wind. His mother died a few days after His birth, and Dad was long gone by then. So Nanabozho was raised by His grandmother Nokomis, the Anishinaabe Earth mother.

It was apparent early on that Nanabozho was special. He could shapeshift, and sometimes appeared as a rabbit, which earned Him the title of the Great Hare. After a series of improbable incidents, including a battle royal with His father, Nanabozho was considered the champion of His people. But He was half-human, and subject to all the usual human frailties: laziness, fear, and so on. However, he was also subject to the best qualities in humanity, as evidenced by this tale from *The Manitous: The Spiritual World of the Ojibway* by Basil Johnston.

Children in those days had nothing to delight them. Sticks, stones, and bugs were all they had to play with, and they soon became depressed. They even stopped smiling. Clearly, something had to be done before they were lost for good.

Their parents did everything they could think of. Finally, out of answers, they turned to their champion, Nanabozho.

Nanabozho didn't know what to do, either, and His appearance scared the kids so much that they screamed and screamed. The parents finally had to ask Him to leave the village.

Poor Nanabozho felt for those kids. And to tell the truth, their reaction had hurt His pride. So He was determined to save them. He climbed the highest mountain, and at the very top, He cried out to Gitchi-Manitou, the Great Spirit, for an answer. The answer He got was cryptic, of course: "Even stones have wings," Gitchi-Manitou said.

Nanabozho thought and thought, but He couldn't figure out the answer to the riddle. As He trudged home, frustrated, He threw a handful of pebbles into the air – and the pebbles changed to colorful butterflies behind Him. Unbeknownst to Nanabozho, the butterflies followed Him home, and they so delighted the children that they began to laugh and play again. Ever since then, the Anishinaabe have considered butterflies to be a symbol of happiness.

Raven

Tlingit – Rafe Orloff – **Dragon's Web**

Ravens figure in myths and legends around the world, and are considered both good and bad, depending on the culture. Odin, the Norse Allfather, has two raven companions who serve as His spies. The Greeks associated ravens with Apollo and considered them to be the god's messengers in the human world. The Irish war goddess Morrigan and her sister goddess, Badb, are also associated with ravens – as is the Welsh god Bran, whose name means "raven."

Ravens figure in more modern legends, too. Guards at the Tower of London take great care with their flock of ravens, for legend has it that if the ravens leave, England will fall. And you may recall a particular raven that Edgar Allen Poe made famous in his spooky poem of the same name.

But ravens and crows get a bad rap. More often than not, they're considered to be harbingers of death, but in reality, they're resourceful and super-smart. Researchers have seen them not just use tools, but create them; the birds will use a sharp blade of grass, for example, to shape a stick into a hook to retrieve a bit of food. In another experiment, a flock of crows not only learned to recognize a particular human face, but taught their young to recognize it, too. And some crows know that if they drop a walnut on the street, a passing car will roll over it and crack it open for them – and furthermore, they know enough to wait until the light turns red to retrieve the nut. Gives a whole new meaning to the word birdbrain, doesn't it?

But here, let me climb down off my soapbox and get on with the business at hand – which, in terms of the *Pipe Woman Chronicles*, is to tell you about Raven the Trickster, who figures prominently in the mythology of tribes of the Pacific Northwest. Here's my favorite Raven tale. It's a Haida legend about how our Trickster friend brought light to the world.

At first, the world was in darkness, and Raven was tired of it. So He went looking for light. Eventually, He discovered that an old man was keeping it tightly sealed in a box. Raven decided to steal it. He thought and thought, and at last, He hit upon a plan.

The old man lived with his daughter in a house near a river. Raven waited until the daughter came to the river to fetch water. He changed himself into a hemlock needle and made sure He got into her water-basket. Then He made sure to get into her mouth when she drank from the basket.

When He reached her belly, he transformed Himself again; three guesses what He changed into.

At last the daughter gave birth. The old man loved the child, but the little one was under strict orders not to touch the old man's treasure box. Raven begged and pleaded to be allowed to hold the light for just a moment, and eventually, He wore the old man down. When the man tossed the glowing sphere of light to Raven, He transformed into His true shape, snatched the sun out of the air with His beak, and flew away through the house's smokehole.

Either He brushed against the smokehole's sooty edges as He left, or the sun singed His feathers as He flew up to place the Sun in the sky. Either way, ever afterward, the people have had light, and Raven has been black.

Tezcatlipoca

Aztec/Mexica – Jack Rivers – **Fissured**

In many regions of the world, conquering or neighboring civilizations adapted cultural figures and practices from one another. For example, the Pueblo Indians taught the Navajo how to weave (although the Navajo say it was Spider Woman who taught them). And Catholicism made a practice – whether deliberately or unconsciously – of conflating local deities with various saints. As I've said before, it's a human trait to look for the familiar in the unfamiliar, and then to proclaim the two the same.

The same thing happened in Mesoamerica. So when we talk about Tezcatlipoca and His brother, Quetzalcoatl, we have to reach back through Aztec history to find their origins in the Olmec and Mayan cultures. By the time the Aztecs came along, Tezcatlipoca had picked up a lot of traits from these earlier cultures, making Him a complex deity.

He and Quetzalcoatl were two of four brothers. Sometimes, all four were referred to as Tezcatlipocas, each representing a different color and a different cardinal direction. But the one we're primarily interested in is the one whose color is black and whose cardinal direction is north. Tezcatlipoca is the Nahuatl word for "smoking mirror," and in fact, our Tezcatlipoca's right foot was replaced by an obsidian mirror; He lost the foot originally in a battle with the Earth Monster. Sometimes His right foot was depicted as a serpent instead, and in that case He would wear the obsidian mirror on His chest or head. He was often shown with yellow and black stripes across His face – a reference, perhaps, to His sacred animal, the jaguar. Among other things, He was associated with the night wind, enmity and discord, rulership, and sorcery.

Today, He and Quetzalcoatl are seen as eternal foes warring for control of the world, with the Feathered Serpent being the god of light, if you will, and Tezcatlipoca serving as the god of darkness and evil. But as Shannon tells Naomi in *Fissured*, some scholars believe Tezcatlipoca to be "the embodiment of change through conflict." Change isn't necessarily evil, any more than the status quo is always good. Sometimes you need a god of chaos to shake up the dominant paradigm and bring the universe back into balance.

Iktomi

Lakota – Webb Curtis – **Firebird's Snare**

Iktomi, whose name means "spider," is considered to be the culture hero of the Sioux. His role is very similar to that of Nanabush for the Anishinaabe, but His origins are somewhat different. Iktomi started out as Ksa, the embodiment of wisdom, but lost that title because of His tendency to be a troublemaker. However, He retained the ability to speak the language of all the people, from humans to trees to rocks.

Like other Tricksters, Iktomi plays the fool in myths told to children to teach them proper ways to behave. Like Coyote, Iktomi makes a lot of elaborate plans to trick people, often involving shapeshifting – and also like Coyote, Iktomi's plans usually backfire spectacularly.

The Ojibwe invented the dreamcatcher, but the Lakota have adapted the design – and as you might expect, they give Iktomi credit for it. The story goes like this: While on a high mountain, an old Lakota shaman was visited by Iktomi in a vision. The god picked up the feathered and beaded willow hoop that the shaman had brought as an offering, and began to spin a web across it. As He worked, He talked to the shaman about the cycle of life – infancy, young adulthood, adulthood, and old age – and about how important it was for people to be guided by good in everything they did. At last, Iktomi showed the shaman the willow hoop. He had left a hole in the middle of the web, and He told the man that good dreams would be caught in the web and kept for the sleeper, while bad dreams would pass through the hole. (For the Ojibwe, it's the other way around: the good dreams pass through and the bad dreams get trapped in the web.)

Speaking of webs, there's a prophecy that Iktomi will one day spread his web across the world. Modern-day Native Americans originally interpreted that to mean telephone lines, but maybe the World Wide Web is a better candidate.

Sacred Clown

Lakota – Webb Curtis – **Dragon's Web**

While we're here in South Dakota, I'll go ahead and explain about the *heyoka*, or Sacred Clown.

Earlier, I mentioned the Wolf Dreamer society of the Sioux. Another Sioux dreaming society is that of the Sacred Clowns, and it works a little differently than the others. As with the other dreaming societies, membership is determined when a particular spirit comes to a man in a dream. In the case of the *heyoka*, the spirit who comes is the Wakinyan – the Thunderbird. I'll talk more about Thunderbirds later, in the Elementals section. But suffice it for now to say that Thunderbirds create thunder with their voices, wind with their great wings, and lightning by opening and closing their eyes.

As you might expect, dreaming of one of these beings could make you a little crazy. And a Sacred Clown is required to act a little crazy: to stand up when it's time to sit, say, or to ride his horse backwards.

This might be fun for a while, but I can imagine it would get old in a hurry. There's one perk of being *heyoka*, though, that might make up for it: like a Druidic bard, a *heyoka* is allowed to make fun of the leaders of the tribe. If he thinks the chief is misguided, he's allowed to say so – and to make everyone laugh while doing it.

As soon as I learned about the close connection between Thunderbirds and Sacred Clowns, I knew exactly which role Webb would play in Sage's life. He had to be the annoying little brother who did crazy stuff like knitting nets for capturing giant iceworms, and who was in charge of speaking truth to Sage's power when the situation called for it.

The kushtaka

*Tlingit – Roberta Newsome – **Firebird's Snare***

You can blame Raven for kushtakas. For the Tlingit and Haida, according to Mary Beck in *Shamans and Kushtakas*, it was Raven who was responsible for organizing human and animal life on Earth. It seems that when He gave otters the ability to live both on land and in the water, He also gave Them the power to create illusions and to shapeshift. In addition, He made Them responsible for rescuing stray humans lost in the woods or at sea.

The Land Otters took Their jobs a little too seriously, to the point where, if they captured a wayward human, they would turn him or her into a kushtaka – half-human, half-Land Otter. It was possible to rescue someone from the Land Otters, but the process required shamanic expertise and wasn't always successful. In short, it was best not to fall afoul of the Land Otters at all.

Kushtakas behaved much like Land Otters. They would lure their victims by shapeshifting into the guise of the person's dead friends or relatives, and by putting a sort of glamor over the victims so the illusions would hold. Sometimes people could see through the glamor; then they might notice the kushtaka's arms growing out of the middle of its chest, instead of out of its shoulders.

Human defenses against a kushtaka attack were few but potent, often involving the use of human blood or urine. In

Firebird's Snare, I invented a magical mudpack for Sage to slather on Rafe while the shaman tried to release the kushtaka's hold on him. It seemed a little less revolting than having somebody pee on the poor guy.

Loki

Norse – Brock Holt – **Seized**

I've already given my speech about my scanty knowledge of the Norse pantheon twice in this book. Maybe three will be the charm?

In a nutshell: I based my depictions of the Norse gods and goddesses on what I remembered from school, a little internet research, and the Marvel Universe movies. In the case of Loki, I also relied on my editor Kat, who was somewhat obsessed with Tom Hiddleston, the actor who plays Loki in the first "Avengers" movie and the first three "Thor" films (the third being in production as I write this).

One thing I decided to do early on (and have tried to be consistent about) was to capitalize pronouns for all of the gods – not just Jehovah and Jesus, but everybody else, too. So Kat and I discussed whether Loki could be considered a god. He wasn't Aesir, or Odin's crew, despite the movie scripts in which Thor and Loki called each other "brother" every few lines. (In Marvel's story line, Odin adopted Loki.) He also wasn't Vanir, the secondary tier of gods and goddesses that included Frey and Freya. He was a Frost Giant, and our feeling was that it made Him a bit of an outsider – particularly because His Trickster nature didn't make Him all that endearing.

I've since heard from a couple of Asatruar – modern Neopagans who follow the Norse gods – who tell me they do, in fact, consider Loki to be a god. By that point, I'd solved the situation: in *Annealed*, Naomi convinced Odin to let Loki out of His eternal torment and rejoin the pantheon. From then on, Loki got His capitalized pronouns and everybody, presumably, was happy.

The thing that got Loki in such trouble was this:

Odin's son Baldur was a handsome, capable fellow who was loved by everyone. But one night, He had a dream that seemed to predict His death. His mother, Frigga, learned of it, and extracted a promise from everything in the realm that it would never harm Baldur. The only thing She didn't bother with was the mistletoe, as She thought it was too weak to threaten anyone.

As soon as Loki heard about it, He set about making a spear out of mistletoe.

In the meantime, it had become quite the sport amongst the warriors in Valhalla to throw stuff at Baldur and watch it all bounce off of Him. While they were having their fun, Loki handed the mistletoe spear to Baldur's blind brother, Hodor, and told him to throw it. Hodor did, and Baldur died.

Once Baldur's body was sent off to sea aboard His flaming ship, His grieving mother persuaded Hel, the goddess of the underworld (the one where people who don't die in battle go), to send Her son back to the land of the living if everything living and dead would weep for Him. Everything did – except for a single giantess, who was rumored to be Loki in disguise.

For His role in Baldur's death, Odin ordered that Loki spend eternity tied, with His own offspring's intestines, to a rock positioned below a serpent whose mouth drips poison. Loki's wife, Sigyn, is allowed to hold a basin between Loki and the serpent – but the basin fills up, and when that happens, She has to move it to empty it. At that point, the acid strikes Loki, and His writhing causes earthquakes.

But Ragnarok is coming. That's when Loki will be freed to lead the Giants against the gods, and Baldur and Hodor will be reunited to rule over the human world – that is, until the next Ragnarok, when the cycle will start over. (And here you thought "everything that has happened before will happen again" was just a Cylon thing.)

Veles

Slavic – Ben Orloff – **Dragon's Web**

Veles, the Slavic god of the underworld, is misunderstood these days. Oh, sure, He's famous for turning Himself into a serpent and hassling Perun until the thunder god gets mad and kills Him – thereby creating the rainstorms that allow everything on Earth to live. But Veles has a softer side, too. He's known in southern Slavic lands as the lord of the forest, protector of everything that lives there – particularly wolves and bears. When He's in human form, Veles sports a pair of bull's or ram's horns. He's also associated with music, wealth, magic, and medicine.

In short, He's not a bad guy – and in fact, after Christianity spread across the Slavic lands, St. Nicholas replaced Veles in many folk tales. His role as a protector of cattle was transferred to St. Blaise. But because of Veles' underworld connections, He was cast as the Devil.

And although I've linked Him in this guide with Rafe's father, please keep in mind that Veles is a Trickster, and the real story may not be the way it appears at first glance. (How's that for a "read and find out"?)

Hermes

*Classical (Greek) – Roman Holt – **Turtle's Weir***

You can blame Hermes on my editor, too. I was musing aloud – well, in an email – about who Roman Holt's god might be, when Susan suggested this guy. I wanted a Classical deity because Roman's mother is Antonia Greco. I suppose I could have paired him with a Norse deity, as his father is affiliated with Loki, but I already had a fair number of Norse gods and goddesses in the series. Anyway, when Susan told me Hermes was a Trickster, it pretty much sealed the deal.

Hermes is the messenger of the gods. He's the one with the little wings on His cap and sandals. He is also considered a god of transitions, and of trade. He sometimes acts as a guide to the Underworld – a useful skill in a companion for Webb as they seek a way into the gods' realm. And He's also known for playing tricks on His fellow gods, sometimes for humanity's sake, but sometimes for His own amusement.

Hermes' equivalent in the Roman pantheon is Mercury, and Roman Holt's quip about wingéd Mercury in *Turtle's Weir* is a reference to a line in Shakespeare's play *Richard III*.

The kappa

*Shinto – Hilary Takahashi – **Dragon's Web***

As I said earlier, there wouldn't be a kappa in this series if it weren't for my editors. When I began planning the first two books of the *Pipe Woman's Legacy*, I wanted Hilary to be Korean-American. I knew Susan had begun studying Korean, so I asked her about possible surnames and about what she knew of their pantheon. It was at about that point when Kat said, "Why don't you make her Japanese-American? Then both Susan and I can help you." The next thing I knew, Hilary had a Japanese name, and I was studying up on kappas.

Here is what I learned: the kappa is a water spirit or demon. The name is a catch-all term that translates to "river child"; there are a whole bunch of regional variations, including *enkō*, which is how Hilary's kappa, Enkou, got his name.

A kappa is about the size of a child when it stands upright. It's described as looking a lot like a turtle, with a duck's beak and a sort of tonsure atop its head. This hairy halo surrounds a depression in the top of the kappa's skull. When the creature leaves water for any length of time, it needs to keep that bowl filled with water, or it will die.

They're mischievous, as befits a Trickster – they like to look up women's kimonos, for one thing. But they've also been accused of drowning people, eating children, and even raping women. However, they're pretty easy to disarm: upon meeting a kappa, bow deeply. The creature will bow in return, and dump all the water out of its head, leaving it paralyzed.

Kappas do speak Japanese, and they've been known to befriend people who give them gifts of certain foods, with cucumbers being their absolute favorite. In fact, they like cucumbers better than human children. Sometimes Japanese parents will throw cucumbers into kappa-infested waters so the family can go in and bathe.

As Tricksters go, kappas are honorable. They will not break an oath, and they are helpful to people when it suits them to be. So it may be worth your while to befriend a kappa. Just be sure to stock up on cucumbers and keep them handy.

Elementals

The spirit Bear whuffed and nudged Darrell with Her head. Clearly, She had claimed him as Her own – for the warrior and the protector that he was.

From *Undertow*

Most of the spirits or deities in the *Pipe Woman Chronicles* books are humanoid in form, at least some of the time. But a few of Them never take a human shape. At the same time, They interact with humans – sometimes helpfully, sometimes not – while displaying a more limited understanding of humans and human events. For lack of a better term, I'm calling them "elementals."

Thunderbird

Lakota – Sage Curtis – **Dragon's Web**

Thunderbird is one of those spirits that a great many Native American tribes have incorporated into their spiritual beliefs. In some tribe's legends, Thunderbird is treated much like any other god – He may appear in human form, in stories about creation or the weather. However, it's the Lakota version of Thunderbird with whom Sage is aligned, and there is nothing touchy-feely about their god at all.

The Great Thunderbird of the Lakota, Wakinyan Tanka, is formless, yet wears clouds. He has huge wings, claws for feet, and no head – only a massive beak that sports rows of pointed teeth. Thunder is His voice; lightning bolts shoot from His eyes. He hates anything dirty or defiled, and wishes to make these things clean and pure again. He also loves truth, and is liable to send a lightning bolt to kill anyone with the temerity to tell a lie while holding the tribe's sacred pipe. His direction is west and His color is black.

The Lakota believe three more Wakinyan correspond to the other cardinal directions. The North Thunderbird is red, the East is yellow, and the South is white. All four of the Thunderbirds live atop a mountain dubbed Harney Peak by whites, in the Black Hills in South Dakota.

When the tribe prepares for the Sun Dance, the men in charge of readying the sacred pole tie a cross of cherry branches to one of the forked sections near the top. That's Thunderbird's nest. Offerings are tied to the crosspieces before the pole is erected for the dance.

I've already talked about the relationship between Thunderbird and the *heyoka*. Check out the section on Sacred Clowns for more information on that.

As I said, a number of Native American tribes believe in Thunderbird. That includes the Ute. And so before we move on, I wanted to share this Fun Fact to Know and Tell: I've read there's a natural rock formation in the shape of a Thunderbird and a massive serpent in the Grand Mesa National Forest, east of Grand Junction, Colorado. The Utes have a legend about this formation. One time, a Ute chief and his son were camped at the base of the mesa. While the chief was away hunting, a thunderbird swooped into camp and stole the son. The chief climbed all the way up to the thunderbird's nest and discovered his son was already dead; in retaliation, he threw the thunderbird's chicks over the cliff, where they were eaten by the great serpent that lived in the river below. When the thunderbird came back, it flew to the river, caught the great serpent in its claws, and rent it into pieces in midair. The chunks, as they fell, created all of the small lakes near the mesa.

Unktechi

*Lakota – none – **Tapped***

Once again, I am embarrassed. In *Tapped*, Shannon has an unpleasant run-in with the Unktechi, Sioux water spirits described to her as oxen. Later, after White Buffalo Calf Pipe Woman has a pointed discussion with the wayward spirits, Shannon calls on the Unktechi for assistance, and They grant it.

I'm not quite sure where I found that information. Because as it turns out, the usual spelling is Unktehi or Unktehila, and the spirit is not an ox at all, but a massive water serpent with a horn on its head. (On the other hand, the *Pipe Woman Chronicles* books are works of fiction. So within the fictional universe of the books, the Lakota could believe in water oxen called Unktechi, couldn't they? Work with me here.)

At the beginning of the world, the Unktehi and Its little followers caused a great flood that threatened to wipe out the people who lived in what's now the Missouri River valley. The people cried to Thunderbird for help, and He and His smaller Thunderbirds shot off all their thunderbolts at the same time. The bolts were so hot that they boiled away all the water, burned all the trees to ash, and killed the Unktehi, burning away their flesh and turning their bones to stone. Today, we call this region the Badlands of South Dakota, and we call the Unktehi's bones dinosaur fossils.

Did you notice the similarities between this myth and that of Perun and Veles? It appears that myths about horned serpents exist in cultures all over the world.

Totems: Frog, Bear, and Otter

*Potawatomi – Darrell Warren – **Crosswind (Frog), Undertow (Bear), Scorched Earth (Otter)***

Long before the coming of whites to the New World, the Anishinaabe were a group of Native American tribes with similar languages that lived near the Atlantic Ocean. Eventually, many of the tribes migrated inland, settling in the upper Midwest of the United States and Canada. During the journey, one group decided to stay in Michigan. That group then split further into three bands: the Ojibwe (also known as the Chippewa), the Ottawa (more properly spelled Odawa), and the Potawatomi (more properly spelled Bodewadmi). Together, they are known as the Confederacy of the Three Fires.

Their split is fairly recent, as these things go, and so their languages and spiritual practices are still pretty similar. So I have felt relatively comfortable in using Basil Johnston's books about the Ojibwe as a basis for Darrell's Potawatomi beliefs and practices in the *Land, Sea, Sky* books. However, for this section I'll be referring to Ojibwe beliefs, just to keep things honest.

Ojibwe society is built around a system of clan totems – animals whose ascribed characteristics the clan either believes it possesses or would like to emulate. The Ojibwe started out with just five totems, and added more later. Totems are also associated with a specific function within the tribal hierarchy: leadership, defense, sustenance, learning, or medicine. As an example, Crane is associated with leadership – but just because you're born into a Crane family, it doesn't mean you'll automatically be a tribal leader. Positions in the tribal hierarchy are neither hereditary nor permanent.

As *Land, Sea, Sky* starts, Darrell's totem is Frog – one of the medicine totems. That made sense because he was training to be a *midew* – a healer. In addition, Frog represents transformation, and that also seemed to fit Darrell as his life took a sudden left turn from healer to warrior.

Later in the series, Darrell picks up Bear as an additional totem. Bear is one of the Ojibwe defense totems – a good choice, I thought, for a Navy SEAL. Her qualities include strength and courage, which would be excellent in a situation involving conflict of any kind.

Finally, I decided Darrell needed to lighten up. So I gave him Otter – another medicine totem – to help him reconcile his warrior nature with his shamanic powers, and to remind him that it's okay to have fun once in a while.

To be honest, I don't know whether it's okay in Potawatomi society to have more than one totem at a time. But I do know Neopagans sometimes request help from a particular bird or animal with whom they don't have a totemic relationship. And sometimes a new totem will announce itself in your life, whether you're interested in answering its particular challenges or not. Given everything Darrell was dealing with, I figured he needed all the help he could get.

The Rest of the Gang

Your madness has left you, Andrew.
Time to join the human race again, I
think.

Brighid, *Tapped*

A few of the deities in the *Pipe Woman Chronicles* cycle don't
fit any of the previous categories in this book – or at least, Their
actions in my story don't. Some are gods and goddesses with
talents other than those we've been discussing up to now; some
are more properly called heroes; and one guy in an Irish chariot
just happened to be passing through.

I should explain something about the term Celtic at the
outset, since a number of these deities are Irish but one is not.
Celt (the "c" is pronounced like a "k", in contrast to the name of
the Boston pro basketball team) is the umbrella term for a
prehistoric people with similar languages who migrated westward

across Europe from their original homeland. That homeland may have been around Hallstatt, Austria, where archaeologists have found some of the oldest Celtic artifacts.

Today's Celtic nations (although some of the nations are regions of other countries) number seven: Ireland; Scotland; Wales; the Isle of Man, which lies in the Irish Sea between Great Britain and Ireland; Cornwall, in the extreme southwest of England; Brittany, on the coast of France; and Galicia, in northwestern Spain. Yes, Spain. Archaeologists and linguists believe the ancestors of the Irish Gaels migrated there from Galicia by boat.

Anyway, there's evidence that a few gods were worshipped in most or all of these lands, with some local variation, but others are tied to a specific region. (Celtic reconstructionism is a branch of Neopaganism that's attempting to bring back the worship of these gods, in part by studying archaeology to try to figure out how their original followers honored Them.)

Brighid

Celtic (Irish) – Shannon McDonough – **Tapped**

One of the most popular and beloved deities in the Celtic pantheon, Brighid is the goddess of poetry, metalcraft, and healing. She has had a remarkable resilience. The early Catholic Church made Her (or an Irish nun named for Her – it's a little unclear) a saint. St. Brighid, or perhaps the pagan goddess Herself, was supposedly a midwife at the birth of Christ. But it's the saint for sure who is credited with weaving the first Brighid's Cross as a teaching aid while converting a dying pagan lord to Christianity.

A society of nineteen devotees of the goddess kept a perpetual flame alive in Her honor at a sacred site in Kildare, Ireland, until the Reformation in the sixteenth century. In 1993, the Brigidine Sisters relit the flame not far from the original site. It still burns there today, at Solas Bhride, a hermitage and outreach center operated by the sisters in Kildare.

In addition, wells all over Ireland are named for Brighid, and people still tie offerings called clooties to trees near these wells.

Some have suggested one aspect of Brighid might be Brigantia, the mother goddess of the Britons. However, Brigantia is more likely related to Boudica (you may have seen it spelled Boadicea), the Iceni tribal chieftess who rallied her badly-outnumbered forces against the Roman occupation of Britain in the 1st century A.D.

Some Neopagans have attempted to fashion Brighid into a tripartite goddess in the Maiden-Mother-Crone mold. I prefer to think of Her as a single brilliant, enthusiastic, and very talented goddess, and that's how I've portrayed Her in the *Pipe Woman Chronicles.*

Lugh

*Celtic (Irish) – none – **Firebird's Snare***

Let's get one thing straight: No matter what you may have read on the intarwebz, Lugh Lámfhada – Lugh of the Long Hand – is not the Irish god of the sun. That honor falls to Bel (who's also called Belenus), the Shining One. Beltane – the notorious festival also known as May Day – honors Bel.

No, Lugh is the Irish god of light – as well as the god of poetry, woodworking, smithcraft, music, magic, and a host of other things, too. His festival is Lughnasadh, otherwise known as Lammas, and is marked at the beginning of August. But Lughnasadh is not even in His honor; Lugh instituted the festival when He was king of the Tuatha Dé Danaan in honor of His mother.

Lugh is a remarkable guy. I love this passage from Lady Gregory's *Gods and Fighting Men*, describing our young man's arrival at the king's court at Tara. (Please note that the eccentric paragraph style is Lady Gregory's, not mine.)

"What are you skilled in?" said the door-keeper; "for no one without an art comes into Tara." "Question me," said Lugh; "I am a carpenter." "We do not want you; we have a carpenter ourselves, Luchtar, son of Luachaid." "Then I am a smith." "We have a smith ourselves, Colum Cuaillemech of the Three New Ways." "Then I am a champion." "That is no use to us; we have a champion before, Ogma, brother to the king." "Question me again," he said; "I am a harper." "That is no use to us; we have a harper ourselves, Abhean, son of Bicelmos, that the Men of the Three Gods brought from the hills." "I am a poet," he said then, "and a teller of tales." "That is no use to us; we have a teller of tales ourselves, Erc, son of Ethaman." "And I am a magician." "That is no use to us; we have plenty of magicians and people of power." "I am a physician," he said. "That is no use; we have Diancecht for our physician." "Let me be a cup-bearer," he said. "We do not want you; we have nine cup-bearers ourselves. "I am a good worker in brass." "We have a worker in brass ourselves, that is Credne Cerd."

Then Lugh said: "Go and ask the king if he has any one man that can do all these things, and if he has, I will not ask to come into Tara."

So the guard goes in and tells Nuada about the fellow at the door. The king orders the chessboards brought out; Lugh takes on all comers and wins every game. At that point, Nuada says He can stay. And a good thing, too, because Lugh goes on to become king of the Tuatha, and fulfills a prophecy by killing His own grandfather, Balor of the Formorians.

You definitely do not want to cross Lugh. When the three sons of Tuireann go hunting one day, they kill Lugh's father, who had taken the shape of a pig at the time. Lugh tracks down the young men and sets for them a series of seemingly impossible tasks that take them all over the known world. Lugh clearly expects the men to die on their quest. But somehow they manage to complete every task and return to Ireland, although mortally wounded. They appeal to Lugh for access to one of the items they had brought back for Him – a magical item that would heal their wounds. The king refuses, and all three men die.

So there you have it: Lugh is a multi-talented god, but don't ever cross Him, if you value your life.

(The story of the sons of Tuireann, by the way, is one of the three great tragedies of Irish mythology. The other two are "Deirdre of the Sorrows," from the Ulster Cycle; and "The Fate of the Children of Lír," which I used as a basis for my YA novel, *SwanSong*.)

Epona

Celtic (Continental) – Kerry Hanrahan – **Dragon's Web**

Epona was originally a Celtic deity whose name means "Great Mare." Her worship was centered in Gaul (a huge swath of Europe encompassing all of present-day France, Belgium, and Luxembourg, as well as most of Switzerland and parts of

Germany, the Netherlands, and northern Italy). The Roman legions became acquainted with Her there and took Her home with them – the only Celtic deity to make the transition to Roman worship.

Epona was a protector of horses, donkeys and mules. She was also a goddess of fertility, and was sometimes portrayed with a mare and a foal.

She may or may not be related to Rhiannon, the Welsh goddess of sovereignty, who makes Her entrance in the *Mabinogion* riding on a white horse. It's a better bet that the English practice of riding hobby-horses on May Day grew from the worship of Epona in ancient times.

Freya

*Norse – none – **Turtle's Weir***

Even if you know very little about Norse mythology (which I've already made clear is true of me), you've almost certainly heard of Freya. She is Frey's sister and the Norse goddess of love. She owns a feathered cloak which allows her to fly; She also has a chariot pulled by two cats. And She wears an amber necklace called Brisingamen. Legend has it that She spotted the necklace while visiting the dwarves who had made it. She asked them to sell it to Her; they responded She could have it if She slept with each of them – which, apparently, She did.

Less well-known is Her ability to practice seidr, a type of Norse shamanism. The shaman uses a ritual distaff, or spindle, to discover a petitioner's destiny and, if necessary, re-weave part of the web. It was Freya, in fact, who brought the art of seidr to the gods.

Hel

*Norse – none – **Annealed***

Hel (whose name is often spelled Hela) makes a brief appearance in *Gravid* when Her father, Loki, pleads with Her to let Him talk to Baldur, Odin's dead son. She is the goddess who rules over Hel, the place where Norse who aren't warriors go when they die. She is often described as looking like a hag, half-alive and half-dead, and is generally indifferent to the desires of humanity – or, apparently, the desires of Her father.

Some scholars think Hel the goddess was created by an ancient poet who was trying to anthropomorphize Hel the underworld. No matter. I suspect Neil Gaiman was right in his novel *American Gods* when he suggested that gods need only to be honored by mortals to attain deific status – so I think we can safely say that wherever Hel the goddess came from, She is worthy of being included in the Norse pantheon now.

Heracles

*Classical (Greek) – none – **Firebird's Snare***

Heracles (whose Roman counterpart was Hercules) didn't start out as a god of the Greek pantheon; he was a hero. His father was Zeus and His mother was a mortal named Alcmene. Zeus's wife Hera wanted the child dead, and even set loose a couple of venomous snakes in His crib. Not long afterward, little Heracles was found to be very much alive, gurgling baby talk to the dead snakes He held tightly in His chubby fists.

He became even stronger as He grew, and went on to star in a bunch of Greek myths. His arch-enemy set Him up with ten impossible Labors to perform. Of course, Heracles completed them all (and with a less bitter fate than the sons of Tuireann). Later, Heracles helped Jason in his search for the Golden Fleece.

Later still, Heracles aided the gods in their war against the Giants. For that, upon His death, They allowed Him to become a full-fledged member of Their pantheon – the only hero to be so honored by the gods.

Probably because of His prodigious strength and courage, the gods call on Heracles to help carve out a vast cavern for Rafe's carbon-capture experiment in *Firebird's Snare.*

Benzaiten

*Shinto – Hilary Takahashi – **Firebird's Snare***

After bringing a Japanese water demon into the *Pipe Woman's Legacy* books, I knew I had to do something to balance things out. That's part of the reason why Hilary ended up with two deities: Enkou the kappa, and Benzaiten, the Shinto goddess of all that flows.

Worship of various deities was as fluid in ancient Asia as it was in the West; cultures rubbed up against each other in war or trade (or both), and borrowed or adapted each other's languages and culture – or had them imposed upon them. Such is likely the case with Benzaiten. Scholars speculate She may be the Japanese equivalent of the Hindu goddess Sarasvati. Each is typically seen holding a type of lute, and both are goddesses of music and knowledge. In addition, Benzaiten is associated with water – water snakes are sacred to Her – and with eloquence, a quality I thought our shy, retiring Hilary could use.

When Benzaiten made the jump to Japan, She eventually was included in the Seven Lucky Gods – the seven gods who are supposed to bring good fortune. Traditionally, They arrive on their treasure-ship on New Year's Day and distribute gifts to those who deserve them.

Columbia

Neopagan – none – **Crosswind**

Atop the dome of the U.S. Capitol is a statue of a woman. She wears a plumed, military-style helmet; in one hand she carries a laurel wreath and the shield of the United States, and in the other she holds a sheathed sword. Staffers in the Capitol Visitors' Center will inform you that the name of the statue is "Freedom," and they might get testy if you question them.

But come on. It's Columbia, the goddess of the United States.

The word "Columbia" was first used to refer to the U.S. in the 1700s; eventually it became a poetic synonym. It's widely used as a place name from sea to shining sea: the capital of South Carolina is called Columbia (as are 19 other U.S. cities and towns), the Columbia River rolls on in the Pacific Northwest, and of course the U.S. capital is located in the District of Columbia. We have Columbia Pictures, the Columbia Broadcasting System (better known these days as CBS), and Columbia University. The 1893 world's fair in Chicago was dubbed the Columbian Exposition.

It wasn't long after coining the term that Columbia began to be personified as a young woman, often depicted in a Native American blanket and feathered headdress. So when Thomas Crawford conceived of his statue of Freedom as draped with a fringed blanket and crowned with feathers in her helmet – well, you see where this is going.

In recent times, Americans have become more comfortable with Lady Liberty as the personification of our country. But Columbia's still around, and some Neopagans have adopted Her as the goddess of the United States. She is certainly a local goddess in D.C. As a lifelong resident of the D.C. area, Sue knew that, and that's why she called on Columbia to help save the city of Washington in *Crosswind*.

Laeg

*Celtic (Irish) – none – **Tapped***

At last, we come to the guy with the chariot.

I'll let you in on a secret: sometimes, authors throw stuff in their books to entertain themselves. That's how Laeg got into *Tapped*. Naomi and Shannon needed to get somewhere in a hurry, and who better to scoop them up and get them there than the greatest Irish charioteer of all time?

Laeg was friend and charioteer to Cuchulainn – son of Lugh, husband to Emer, and the hero of the Ulster Cycle of Irish legends, the most famous of those being *The Cattle Raid of Cooley*. Cuchulainn's birth name was Setanta. But when he was a boy, he accidentally killed a guard dog owned by a man named Culainn. He offered to atone by acting as Culainn's watchdog until a replacement dog could be reared – and was forever after known as Cuchulainn, or the hound of Culainn.

Laeg was quite the hero in his own right, with a history of plucking his friend and master out of scrapes in the nick of time. He also did a fair amount of kidding around with Cuchulainn – just the thing a hero would need to keep him sane.

Now that you have that background, perhaps you can better appreciate Laeg's rescue of Naomi and Shannon in *Tapped*. Especially if you can picture Joseph as a guard dog.

At that very moment, strong hands nabbed us both by the backs of our coats and hauled us into a wagon. A very fast, two-wheeled wagon.

The driver lashed the reins, the horses reared, and we were off.

The pain in my chest dissipated as our distance from the wall increased. Shannon seemed to be recovering, too; she sat up and shook her head. Then she squinted at our rescuer, and her mouth dropped open. "Laeg?" she gasped.

"Ach, so you know me!" the driver cried, pleased. "Lugh sent me. He bade me look out for His daughter-in-law, Emer." He indicated me with a thrust of his chin.

I blinked. "Whoever this Lou is, he must be mistaken," I yelled above the chariot's clatter. "I'm not married. And my name's Naomi."

"Ah," the charioteer grinned, "but are you not the Hound's mate?"

A smile dawned upon Shannon's face. "She is, to be sure."

I frowned a question at Shannon; she waved her hand in a *just roll with it* gesture. I would have thrown up my own hands in surrender, except that I was holding on to the side of the chariot for dear life.

Shannon, bless her heart, knew her mythology. And now, having read this far, so do you – at least as it pertains to the *Pipe Woman Chronicles*.

Conclusion

What am I saying? Am I buying into all of this craziness?

Naomi Witherspoon, *Seized*

Myths which are believed in tend to become true.

George Orwell

I've had fun romping again through the motley collection of pantheons that has ended up in Naomi's world. My heartfelt thanks go to my editors, Susan Strayer and Kat Milyko, who likely had no idea what they were getting into when they agreed to read *Seized*; to Leland Dirks, who suggested that I write a book like this one before putting the series to bed; to the gang around the gruel cauldron at Indies Unlimited; and to the members of my Woo-Woo Team, for their enthusiasm and support.

If you got here via an interest in mythology and non-Western religions, I hope you've enjoyed my take on the deities who appear in the series.

If you're a first-time visitor to the *Pipe Woman Chronicles* universe, I hope this guide has piqued your interest in the novels. I tried not to include any spoilers, but when you're talking about twelve books that span thirty-plus years of time-in-world, it's virtually impossible not to give something away. (For example, I pretty much had to admit that Naomi and Joseph get married and have kids. Sorry.) You can find all of the books on my Amazon author page, as well as omnibus editions for the original five *Pipe Woman Chronicles* books and the *Land, Sea, Sky* trilogy. An omnibus for the *Pipe Woman's Legacy* will be published in November 2016.

If you've enjoyed *A Billion Gods and* Goddesses and would like to know more about my future publishing plans, please sign up for my mailing list at http://eepurl.com/xxw9D, where I share information about all of my new books. I promise not to spam you. If you're already on the mailing list, a thousand blessings upon you.

One more request: If you liked this book – or any of my other books – please think about going back to the place where you bought it and leaving a review. And you're always welcome to drop me a line at lynne.cantwell@hearth-myth.com.

In 2011, in preparation for writing *Seized*, I thought a lot about how our culture – particularly American culture – has gone wrong by celebrating wealth and fame to the detriment of everything else. I even started a discussion at Kevinswatch.com about greed, and about how we might discourage people from indulging in it. That has typically been the purview of religion – but at least in the West, such discouragement has usually taken the form of proscription (which works about as well as someone telling you not to think of a pickle, and for pretty much the same reason), although sometimes it's been stood on its head instead ("God wants you to be rich!").

Then I thought about all of the religions and cultures around the world that have a story – a *myth* – about a savior who will return someday and redeem the true believers. Sometimes the savior is expected to smite their oppressors; sometimes he or she is simply in charge of whisking the faithful up to heaven.

The myth of White Buffalo Woman is one of these. It ends with Her promise that She will be back someday. So in this series, I brought Her back. I brought *all* of the gods back. And then I let Them knock some heads and sort things out.

Do the gods exist? Everyone has their own opinion, and I'm not going to try to convince you that mine is the only one that's right. But I'll leave you, if I may, with one more quote.

I believe in everything until it's disproved. So I believe in fairies, the myths, dragons. It all exists, even if it's in your mind. Who's to say that dreams and nightmares aren't as real as the here and now?

John Lennon

Appendices

Appendices

Appendix A: The A-to-Z List of Gods and Goddesses in the *Pipe Woman Chronicles*

The *Pipe Woman Chronicles* cycle spans twelve books, thirty-odd years, and a whole lot of pantheons. So I've included the following list, alphabetized by name of deity, for readers who are trying to place a particular god or goddess in the context of the story. For each deity, I've included the pantheon, the character with whom they're associated, and the first book in which they appear.

You will sometimes see two (or more) pantheons listed for a deity. The first pantheon is the one in which I have placed the deity for the purposes of my story. The exception is the Aztec/Mexica deities, for which I have put Aztec first because it's the more common term, even though Mexica is more technically correct.

Bear Mother, Tlingit, Sandy Hanlon (mother of Rafe Orloff), *Dragon's Web: Book One of the Pipe Woman's Legacy*

Bear totem, Potawatomi, Darrell Warren, *Undertow: Land, Sea, Sky Book 2*

Benzaiten, Shinto, Hilary Takahashi, *Firebird's Snare: Book Two of the Pipe Woman's Legacy*

Blood Clot Boy, Ute, Looks Far Guzmán, *Seized: Book One of the Pipe Woman Chronicles*

Brighid, Celtic, Shannon McDonough, *Tapped: Book Three of the Pipe Woman Chronicles*

Cerridwen, Celtic, Sage Curtis, *Firebird's Snare: Book Two of the Pipe Woman's Legacy*

Coatlicue, Aztec/Mexica, none, *Annealed: Book Five of the Pipe Woman Chronicles*

Columbia, Neopagan, none, *Crosswind: Land, Sea, Sky Book 1*

Coyote, Ute (but appears in numerous Native American pantheons), Joseph Curtis, *Seized: Book One of the Pipe Woman Chronicles*

Diana, Classical (Roman), Antonia Greco, *Gravid: Book Four of the Pipe Woman Chronicles*

Enkou (a kappa), Shinto, Hilary Takahashi, *Dragon's Web: Book One of the Pipe Woman's Legacy*

Epona, Celtic, Kerry McDonough, *Dragon's Web: Book One of the Pipe Woman's Legacy*

Freya, Norse, none, *Turtle's Weir: Book Four of the Pipe Woman's Legacy*

Frigga, Norse, none, *Tapped: Book Three of the Pipe Woman Chronicles*

Frog totem, Potawatomi, Darrell Warren, *Undertow: Land, Sea, Sky Book 2*

Gaia, Neopagan/Classical (Greek), Sue Killeen, *Crosswind: Land, Sea, Sky Book 1*

Goddess of the Trees, Neopagan, Kalindra (High Priestess of the Grove of the Divine Spark), *Gravid: Book Four of the Pipe Woman Chronicles*

Hel, Norse, none, *Annealed: Book Five of the Pipe Woman Chronicles*

Heracles, Classical (Greek), none, *Firebird's Snare: Book Two of the Pipe Woman's Legacy*

Hermes, Classical (Greek), Roman Holt, *Turtle's Weir: Book Four of the Pipe Woman's Legacy*

Iktomi, Lakota, Webb Curtis, *Firebird's Snare: Book Two of the Pipe Woman's Legacy*

Ingun, Norse, Ingrid Ingunnardottir, *Turtle's Weir: Book Four of the Pipe Woman's Legacy*

Kappa (see Enkou in this list)

Kushtaka, Tlingit, Roberta Newsome, *Firebird's Snare: Book Two of the Pipe Woman's Legacy*

Laeg, Irish (Celtic), none, *Tapped: Book Three of the Pipe Woman Chronicles*

Loki, Norse, Brock Holt, *Seized: Book One of the Pipe Woman Chronicles*

Lugh, Celtic (Irish), none, *Firebird's Snare: Book Two of the Pipe Woman's Legacy*

Morrigan, Celtic (Irish), Tess Showalter, *Crosswind: Land, Sea, Sky Book 1*

Nanabush (Nanabozho), Ojibwe, Darrell Warren, *Crosswind: Land, Sea, Sky Book 1*

Odin, Norse, none, *Seized: Book One of the Pipe Woman Chronicles*

Otter totem, Potawatomi, Darrell Warren, *Undertow: Land, Sea, Sky Book 2*

Oya, Yoruba, Adio Ogwu (Yoruban representative at the big mediation), *Annealed: Book Five of the Pipe Woman Chronicles*

Pele, Hawaiian, Nick Higoshi (Hawaiian representative at the big mediation), *Annealed: Book Five of the Pipe Woman Chronicles*

Perun, Slavic, Paul Orloff, *Dragon's Web: Book One of the Pipe Woman's Legacy*

Quetzalcoatl, Aztec/Mexica, none, *Fissured: Book Two of the Pipe Woman Chronicles*

Rainbow Serpent, Australian Aboriginal, Merindah O'Connor (Aboriginal representative at the big mediation), *Annealed: Book Five of the Pipe Woman Chronicles*

Raven, Tlingit (but appears in numerous Native American pantheons), Rafe Orloff, *Dragon's Web: Book One of the Pipe Woman's Legacy*

Sacred Clown, Lakota, Webb Curtis, *Dragon's Web: Book One of the Pipe Woman's Legacy*

Spider Woman, Navajo, Webb Curtis, *Spider's Lifeline: Book Three of the Pipe Woman's Legacy*

Tezcatlipoca, Aztec/Mexica, Jack Rivers, *Fissured: Book Two of the Pipe Woman Chronicles*

Thor, Norse, Kurt Lange, *Fissured: Book Two of the Pipe Woman Chronicles*

Thunderbird, Lakota (but appears in numerous Native American pantheons), Sage Curtis, *Dragon's Web: Book One of the Pipe Woman's Legacy*

<u>Unktechi</u>, Lakota, none, *Tapped: Book Three of the Pipe Woman Chronicles*

<u>Veles</u>, Slavic, Ben Orloff, *Dragon's Web: Book One of the Pipe Woman's Legacy*

<u>White Buffalo Calf Pipe Woman</u>, Lakota, Naomi Witherspoon Curtis, *Seized: Book One of the Pipe Woman Chronicles*

<u>Wolf Dreamer</u>, Lakota, Andrew Sauvage, *Tapped: Book Three of the Pipe Woman Chronicles*

Appendix B: The Deities by the Books

For brand-new readers of the Pipe Woman Chronicles, I've sorted the list of deities by the name of the book in which They make Their first appearance.

Seized: Book One of the Pipe Woman Chronicles

White Buffalo Calf Pipe Woman, Lakota, Naomi Witherspoon

Coyote, Ute, Joseph Curtis

Odin, Norse, none

Loki, Norse, Brock Holt

Blood Clot Boy, Ute, Looks Far Guzmán

Fissured: Book Two of the Pipe Woman Chronicles

Tezcatlipoca, Aztec/Mexica, Jack Rivers

Thor, Norse, none

Quetzalcoatl, Aztec/Mexica, none

Tapped: Book Three of the Pipe Woman Chronicles

Wolf Dreamer, Lakota, Andrew Sauvage

Unktechi, Lakota, none

Laeg, Irish (Celtic), none

Brighid, Celtic (Irish), Shannon McDonough

Frigga, Norse, none

Gravid: Book Four of the Pipe Woman Chronicles

The Goddess of the Trees, Neopagan, Kalindra (High Priestess of the Grove of the Divine Spark)

Annealed: Book Five of the Pipe Woman Chronicles

Coatlicue, Aztec/Mexica, none

Hel, Norse, none

Pele, Hawaiian, Nick Higoshi

Rainbow Serpent, Australian Aboriginal, Merindah O'Connor

Oya, Yoruba, Adio Ogwu

Crosswind: Land, Sea, Sky Book 1

Nanabush, Ojibwe, Darrell Warren

Frog totem, Potawatomi, Darrell Warren

Morrigan, Celtic (Irish), Tess Showalter

Gaia, Neopagan/Classical (Greek), Sue Killeen

Undertow: Land, Sea, Sky Book 2

Bear totem, Potawatomi, Darrell Warren

Scorched Earth: Land, Sea, Sky Book 3

Otter totem, Potawatomi, Darrell Warren

Dragon's Web: Book One of the Pipe Woman's Legacy

Epona, Celtic (Continental), Kerry Hanrahan

Thunderbird, Lakota, Sage Curtis

Sacred Clown, Lakota, Webb Curtis

Raven, Tlingit, Rafe Orloff

Enkou (a kappa), Shinto, Hilary Takahashi

Perun, Slavic, Paul Orloff (Rafe's brother)

Bear Mother, Tlingit, Sadie Hanlon (Rafe's mother)

Veles, Slavic, Ben Orloff (Rafe's father)

Firebird's Snare: Book Two of the Pipe Woman's Legacy

Benzaiten, Shinto, Hilary Takahashi

Iktomi, Lakota, Webb Curtis

Cerridwen, Celtic (Welsh), Sage Curtis

The kushtaka, Tlingit, Roberta Newsome

Lugh, Celtic (Irish), none

Heracles, Classical (Greek), none

Spider's Lifeline: Book Three of the Pipe Woman's Legacy

Spider Woman, Navajo, Webb Curtis

Turtle's Weir: Book Four of the Pipe Woman's Legacy

Freya, Norse, none

Ingun, Norse, Ingrid Ingunnardottir

Hermes, Classical (Greek), Roman Holt

Appendix C: The Deities by Pantheon

Finally, here is a list of all the gods and goddesses in the series, sorted by pantheon.

Lakota

<u>Iktomi</u>, Webb Curtis, *Firebird's Snare: Book Two of the Pipe Woman's Legacy*

<u>Sacred Clown</u>, Webb Curtis, *Dragon's Web: Book One of the Pipe Woman's Legacy*

<u>Thunderbird</u>, Sage Curtis, *Dragon's Web: Book One of the Pipe Woman's Legacy*

<u>Unktechi</u>, none, *Tapped: Book Three of the Pipe Woman Chronicles*

<u>White Buffalo Calf Pipe Woman</u>, Naomi Witherspoon Curtis, *Seized: Book One of the Pipe Woman Chronicles*

<u>Wolf Dreamer</u>, Andrew Sauvage, *Tapped: Book Three of the Pipe Woman Chronicles*

Ute:

Blood Clot Boy, Looks Far Guzmán, *Seized: Book One of the Pipe Woman Chronicles*

Coyote, Joseph Curtis, *Seized: Book One of the Pipe Woman Chronicles*

Ojibwe and/or Potawatomi

Bear totem, Darrell Warren, *Undertow: Land, Sea, Sky Book 2*

Frog totem, Darrell Warren, *Crosswind: Land, Sea, Sky Book 1*

Nanabush (Nanabozho), Darrell Warren, *Crosswind: Land, Sea, Sky Book 1*

Otter totem, Potawatomi, Darrell Warren, *Scorched Earth: Land, Sea, Sky Book 3*

Aztec (Mexica)

Coatlicue, none, *Annealed: Book Five of the Pipe Woman Chronicles*

Quetzalcoatl, none, *Fissured: Book Two of the Pipe Woman Chronicles*

Tezcatlipoca, Jack Rivers, *Fissured: Book Two of the Pipe Woman Chronicles*

Tlingit

Bear Mother, Sandy Hanlon (mother of Rafe Orloff), *Dragon's Web: Book One of the Pipe Woman's Legacy*

Kushtaka, Roberta Newsome, *Firebird's Snare: Book Two of the Pipe Woman's Legacy*

Raven, Rafe Orloff, *Dragon's Web: Book One of the Pipe Woman's Legacy*

Hawaiian

Pele, Nick Higoshi (Hawaiian representative at the big mediation), *Annealed: Book Five of the Pipe Woman Chronicles*

Navajo

Spider Woman, Webb Curtis, *Spider's Lifeline: Book Three of the Pipe Woman's Legacy*

Norse

Freya, none, *Turtle's Weir: Book Four of the Pipe Woman's Legacy*

Frigga, none, *Tapped: Book Three of the Pipe Woman Chronicles*

Hel, none, *Annealed: Book Five of the Pipe Woman Chronicles*

Ingun, Ingrid Ingunnardottir, *Turtle's Weir: Book Four of the Pipe Woman's Legacy*

Loki, Brock Holt, *Seized: Book One of the Pipe Woman Chronicles*

Odin, none, *Seized: Book One of the Pipe Woman Chronicles*

Thor, Kurt Lange, *Fissured: Book Two of the Pipe Woman Chronicles*

Celtic

Brighid, Shannon McDonough, *Tapped: Book Three of the Pipe Woman Chronicles*

Cerridwen, Sage Curtis, *Firebird's Snare: Book Two of the Pipe Woman's Legacy*

Epona, Kerry McDonough, *Dragon's Web: Book One of the Pipe Woman's Legacy*

Laeg, none, *Tapped: Book Three of the Pipe Woman Chronicles*

Lugh, none, *Firebird's Snare: Book Two of the Pipe Woman's Legacy*

Morrigan, Celtic, *Tess Showalter, Crosswind: Land, Sea, Sky Book 1*

Classical (Greek/Roman)

Diana, Antonia Greco, *Gravid: Book Four of the Pipe Woman Chronicles*

Heracles, none, *Firebird's Snare: Book Two of the Pipe Woman's Legacy*

Hermes, Roman Holt, *Turtle's Weir: Book Four of the Piew Woman's Legacy*

Slavic

Perun, Paul Orloff, *Dragon's Web: Book One of the Pipe Woman's Legacy*

Veles, Ben Orloff, *Dragon's Web: Book One of the Pipe Woman's Legacy*

Shinto

Benzaiten, Hilary Takahashi, *Firebird's Snare: Book Two of the Pipe Woman's Legacy*

Enkou (a kappa), Hilary Takahashi, *Dragon's Web: Book One of the Pipe Woman's Legacy*

Yoruba

Oya, Adio Ogwu (Yoruban representative at the big mediation), *Annealed: Book Five of the Pipe Woman Chronicles*

Australian Aboriginal

Rainbow Serpent, Merindah O'Connor (Aboriginal representative at the big mediation), *Annealed: Book Five of the Pipe Woman Chronicles*

Neopagan

Columbia, none, *Crosswind: Land, Sea, Sky Book 1*

Gaia, Sue Killeen, *Crosswind: Land, Sea, Sky Book 1*

Goddess of the Trees, Kalindra (High Priestess of the Grove of the Divine Spark), *Gravid: Book Four of the Pipe Woman Chronicles*

Further Reading

Novelists pull ideas and inspiration from all over the place when creating the characters in their books, usually with little thought to retreading the same ground to create a work of nonfiction. So I have not kept track of all the websites I've consulted while doing research for the *Pipe Woman Chronicles*. In any case, some have been more helpful than others. (You know what Abraham Lincoln said: You can't trust everything you read on the internet.)

Still, I will admit to consulting a few sites fairly regularly, as springboards for further research: Wikipedia, native-languages.org, and Godchecker.com (which is always entertaining, if not chock-full of facts). Beyond that, Google has been my friend on more occasions than I can count.

Printed references are easier to keep track of. Here's a list of some of the books I used while writing the *Pipe Woman Chronicles* cycle:

Allen, Paula Gunn. *Grandmothers of the Light: A Medicine Woman's Sourcebook*. Boston: Beacon Press, 1991. ISBN: 0-8070-8103-5.

---. *The Sacred Hoop: Recovering the Feminine in American Indian Traditions*. Boston: Beacon Press, 1992. ISBN: 0-8070-4617-5.

Augusta, Lady Gregory. *Cuchulain of Muirthemne*. Mineola, NY: Dover Publications, 2001. ISBN: 0-486-41717-4.

—. *Gods and Fighting Men*. Gerrards Cross, UK: Guernsey Press Co. Ltd., 1999. ISBN: 0-901072-37-0.

Beck, Mary G. *Heroes & Heroines in Tlingit-Haida Legend*. Seattle: Alaska Northwest Books, 1990. ISBN: 0-88240-334-6.

—. *Potlatch: Native Ceremony and Myth on the Northwest Coast*. Seattle: Alaska Northwest Books, 1993. ISBN: 0-88240-440-7.

—. *Shamans and Kushtakas: North Coast Tales of the Supernatural*. Seattle: Alaska Northwest Books, 1991. ISBN: 0-88240-406-7.

Beckwith, Martha. *Hawaiian Mythology*. Honolulu: University of Hawaii Press, 1970. ISBN: 0-8248-0514-3.

Bell, Ellen. *Daughters of the Dreaming*, 3rd ed. North Melbourne, Australia: Spinifex Press, 2002. ISBN: 1-87675-615-2.

Dundes, Alan, ed. *Sacred Narrative: Readings in the Theory of Myth*. Berkeley, CA: University of California Press, 1984. ISBN: 0-520-05192-0.

Erdoes, Richard, and Alfonso Ortiz, eds. *American Indian Myths and Legends*. New York: Pantheon Books, 1984. ISBN: 0-394-74018-1.

Ford, Clyde W. *The Hero with an African Face: Mythic Wisdom of Traditional Africa*. New York: Bantam Books, 2000. ISBN: 0-553-37868-6.

Johnston, Basil. *The Manitous: The Spiritual World of the Ojibway*. St. Paul, MN: Minnesota Historical Society Press, 2001. ISBN: 0-87351-411-4.

—. *Honour Earth Mother*. Lincoln, NE: University of Nebraska Press, 2003. ISBN: 0-8032-7622-2.

—. *Ojibway Ceremonies*. Lincoln, NE: University of Nebraska Press, 1990. ISBN: 0-8032-7573-0.

—. *Ojibway Heritage*. Lincoln, NE: University of Nebraska Press, 1990. ISBN: 0-8032-7572-2.

Leeming, David. *A Dictionary of Asian Mythology*. New York: Oxford University Press, 2001. ISBN: 0-19-512053-1.

Lindow, John. *Norse Mythology: A Guide to Gods, Heroes, Rituals, and Beliefs*. New York: Oxford University Press, 2001. ISBN: 0-19-515382-0.

Mails, Thomas E. *Plains Indians: Dog Soldiers, Bear Men and Buffalo Women*. New York: Prentice-Hall, Inc., 1973. ISBN: 0-88394-082-5.

Mbiti, John S. *African Religions and Philosophy*. Garden City, NY: Anchor Books, 1970. ISBN: 0-385-03713-9.

Miller, Mary, and Karl Taube. *An Illustrated Dictionary of the Gods and Symbols of Ancient Mexico and the Maya*. London: Thames & Hudson Inc., 1993. ISBN: 978-0-500-27928-1.

Powers, William K. *Oglala Religion*. Lincoln, NE: University of Nebraska Press, 1975. ISBN: 0-8032-8706-2.

Puhvel, Jaan. *Comparative Mythology*. Baltimore, MD: The Johns Hopkins University Press, 1987. ISBN: 9780801839382.

Read, Kay Almere, and Jason J. Gonzalez. *Mesoamerican Mythology: A Guide to the Gods, Heroes, Rituals, and Beliefs of Mexico and Central America*. Santa Barbara, CA: Oxford University Press, 2000. ISBN: 0-19-514909-2.

Smith, Anne M. *Ute Tales*. Salt Lake City, UT: University of Utah Press, 1992. ISBN: 0-87480-442-6.

Wroth, William, ed. *Ute Indian Arts & Culture: From Prehistory to the New Millennium*. Colorado Springs, CO: Colorado Springs Fine Arts Center, 2000. ISBN: 0-916537-12-9.

About the Author

Lynne Cantwell writes mostly urban fantasy and paranormal romance, with a dash of magic realism when she's feeling more serious. She is also a contributing author for Indies Unlimited. In a previous life, she was a broadcast journalist who worked at Mutual/NBC Radio News, CNN, and a bunch of other places you have probably never heard of. She has a master's degree in fiction writing from Johns Hopkins University. Currently, she lives near Washington, D.C.

The Pipe Woman Chronicles Universe

Seized: Book One of the Pipe Woman Chronicles
Fissured: Book Two of the Pipe Woman Chronicles
Tapped: Book Three of the Pipe Woman Chronicles
Gravid: Book Four of the Pipe Woman Chronicles
Annealed: Book Five of the Pipe Woman Chronicles
The Pipe Woman Chronicles Omnibus (only for Kindle)
Where Were You When: A Land, Sea, Sky Anthology
Crosswind: Land, Sea, Sky Book 1
Undertow: Land, Sea, Sky Book 2
Scorched Earth: Land, Sea, Sky Book 3
The Land Sea Sky Trilogy (only for Kindle)
Dragon's Web: Book One of the Pipe Woman's Legacy
Firebird's Snare: Book Two of the Pipe Woman's Legacy
Spider's Lifeline: Book Three of the Pipe Woman's Legacy
Turtle's Weir: Book Four of the Pipe Woman's Legacy

The Stand-alone Novels

The Maidens' War
SwanSong
Seasons of the Fool

Short Stories
Back Home Again: The Five59 Stories, plus a few

Contributor
Indies Unlimited 2012 Flash Fiction Anthology
Indies Unlimited 2013 Flash Fiction Anthology
Indies Unlimited 2014 Flash Fiction Anthology
Indies Unlimited Tutorials and Tools for Prospering in a Digital World
Indies Unlimited Tutorials and Tools for Prospering in a Digital World, Vol. II
BookGoodies How to Write A Book
First Chapters
13 Bites
Summer Dreams
Boo!: Volume 2
Winter Tales
Other Realms
Plan 559 from Outer Space
13 Bites Vol. III
I Heard It on the Radio
Plan 559 from Outer Space Mk. II

Find Lynne on Teh Intarwebz:
Facebook: http://www.facebook.com/pages/Lynne-Cantwell
Twitter: http://twitter.com/lynnecantwell
Google Plus: http://plus.google.com/+LynneCantwell
Pinterest: http://pinterest.com/LynneCantwell
Goodreads:
http://www.goodreads.com/author/show/696603.Lynne_Cantwell
Blog: http://www.hearth-myth.com

The Books of the *Pipe Woman Chronicles* Cycle

Available from all major online booksellers – or ask your local bookstore to order your copy today!

The Original Series

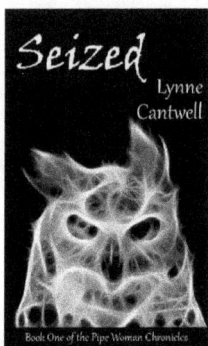

Seized
Lynne Cantwell
Book One of the Pipe Woman Chronicles
ISBN 9781475095524

Naomi Witherspoon has a pretty sweet life. Respected as a skilled mediator, she has an almost uncanny knack for getting people on both sides of a dispute to agree. And her handsome boyfriend Brock has just proposed to her. But a white buffalo calf is bowing to her in her dreams. And who is the Native American man who has been following her around?

Naomi doesn't know it, but her sweet life is about to change.

If anything can go wrong…

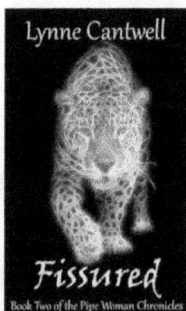

Lynne Cantwell
Fissured
Book Two of the Pipe Woman Chronicles
ISBN 9781479149780

Just as Naomi and Joseph begin to work out their relationship, they meet Jack, filmmaker and candidate for Investigator – but he's not much of a team player. A friend's ranch might be in danger from a new hydraulic fracturing facility. And a jaguar is stalking the banks of Cherry Creek. When the owner of the fracking facility turns out to be an old acquaintance, Naomi begins to wonder how many Tricksters it takes to make a divine deal.

Ah, winter in South Dakota…

Naomi's caught some kind of bug, and she hasn't seen Joseph in weeks. But she lets her best friend, Shannon, drag her on vacation: a road trip to the Pine Ridge Indian Reservation to find Naomi's father. There, they find more than they bargained for: a dream wolf, a mysterious walled compound that might or might not belong to Loki, and a *lot* of snow.

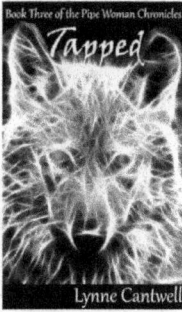

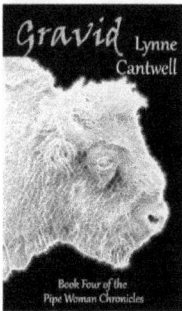

ISBN 97812481153881

Naomi has any number of things she doesn't want to think about: she's pregnant and due any day; Joseph's grandfather needs a new place to live, but he won't move; and a Mexican drug lord's thugs are in town, looking for Jack. But what Naomi's really dodging is a talk with her mother.

If she can negotiate this minefield, mediating an agreement between White Buffalo Calf Pipe Woman and Jehovah ought to be a piece of cake.

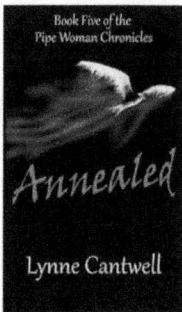

ISBN 9781483918341

It's zero hour...

In this fifth and final book of the original Pipe Woman Chronicles, Naomi is in a race against the clock to balance the demands of her body, her family, and her friends – and she must do it while the whole world is watching.

ISBN 9781489513854

Land, Sea, Sky

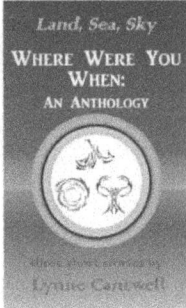

Land, Sea, Sky
WHERE WERE YOU
WHEN:
AN ANTHOLOGY

Lynne Cantwell

eBook Only

On the day when all the pagan gods and goddesses returned to Earth, three of Them -- the Irish war goddess Morrigan, the Wiccan Earth goddess Gaia, and the Ojibwe culture hero Nanabush -- marked three humans as their avatars. Soon, the gods will need them to protect the world They have created from those who profited during the days when Earth was ruled by greed and fear. The three stories in this anthology tell how it all began.

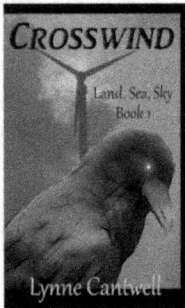

CROSSWIND

Land, Sea, Sky
Book 1

Lynne Cantwell

ISBN 9781494261092

Storm's coming...

Life on Earth is much improved since the pagan gods' return. As conflict has eased around the world, more money is being spent on humanitarian goals. But the former ruling class is about to stage a last-ditch effort to bring the old system back.

In response, the gods have recruited three humans to help Them fight back. But Tess, Darrell and Sue must find a way past their own flaws first.

Surf's up…

Navy Lt. Darrell Warren thinks he's being sent to investigate a terrorist threat against a critical bridge-tunnel. Instead, his commander orders him to infiltrate the terrorists. And he must do it without his housemates – Sue's on vacation and Tess is chasing a hurricane. When all three end up in Virginia Beach on Labor Day, you can bet the gods want Darrell to succeed. But will that be enough?

ISBN 9781497376267

Harvest's in...

Ayalendo: a miracle grain that could end world hunger -- and Lucifer's end game. He plans to control the world's food supply, using hunger as leverage to gain enough followers to allow him to attain godhood. Once again, the gods turn to Tess, Sue, and Darrell to foil the plot and defeat Lucifer, once and for all.

ISBN 9781500149123

Pipe Woman's Legacy

ISBN 9780692452646

Can a god go crazy?

Sage Curtis, reluctant Savior of the Earth, has been yanked around by the gods her whole life. She wants nothing more than to fix Earth's climate with science - not the magic she is capable of. But Veles, the god of the Slavic underworld, has other ideas. One thing is clear: to win, Sage will have to learn how to fly.

ISBN 9780692480243

This is no time for a learning experience...

Sage Curtis is almost reconciled to the idea that she will have to use her Thunderbird powers to reverse climate change -- even though those powers haven't been very helpful so far. But the gods have said if humanity can't fix the climate, They will destroy the planet and start over.

Sage must use both science and magic to save the Earth - and even that may not be enough.

Webb Curtis lives in anticipation.

His relatives do amazing things as a matter of course. But Webb? Knitting is his superpower. He also knows the future, but only when he's not directly involved. Now thirty-five and with a baby on the way, he is trying to find his place in the world. But his task will be complicated by a smoky interloper, an Icelandic princess, a tiny golden spider -- and Ragnarok, a.k.a. the end of the world. Not even Webb himself could have anticipated this...

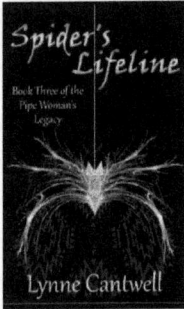

ISBN 9780692688878

FOCUS.

Webb Curtis has a number of urgent projects on his plate. He's supposed to be studying mediation techniques so he can help his mother negotiate a new peace agreement among the gods. He's also supposed to be tracking down the goddess responsible for his mother's illness – and to do that, he needs to find a new way into the gods' realm, as Loki has locked it down while He nudges His fellow gods and goddesses toward Ragnarok. But Webb isn't doing any of that. And he can't remember why.

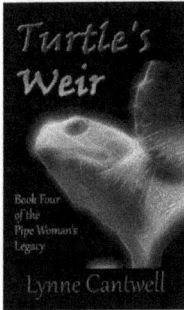

ISBN 9780692751909

What he needs is a whack upside the head…